THE
RULES
ACCORDING TO
JWOWW

THE RULES
ACCORDING TO
JWOWW

JENNI JWOWW FARLEY
WITH SHERYL BERK

• •

Shore-Tested Secrets on Landing a Mint Guy,
Staying Fresh to Death, and Kicking the
Competition to the Curb

WILLIAM MORROW
An Imprint of HarperCollinsPublishers

For my dad, who always believed in me

THE RULES ACCORDING TO JWOWW. Copyright © 2011 by Jenni Farley. Photography © 2011 by Jan Cobb Photography. All rights reserved. Printed in the United States of America. No part of this book may be used or reproduced in any manner whatsoever without written permission except in the case of brief quotations embodied in critical articles and reviews. For information address HarperCollins Publishers, 10 East 53rd Street, New York, NY 10022.

HarperCollins books may be purchased for educational, business, or sales promotional use. For information please write: Special Markets Department, HarperCollins Publishers, 10 East 53rd Street, New York, NY 10022.

FIRST EDITION

Library of Congress Cataloging-in-Publication Data is available upon request.

ISBN 978-0-06-207539-0

11 12 13 14 15   OV/RRD   10 9 8 7 6 5 4 3 2 1

CONTENTS

CONTENTS

CONTENTS

CHAPTER 1

INTRODUCTION

Men may be from Mars and women from Venus, but I'm from the *Jersey Shore*. Down here we do things our own way. These are my rules on dating, JWOWW's rules . . .

Women need dating rules like they need bras. Sure, you can go without them, but if you do—and you're sporting a nice boob job like I am—you are gonna be flopping out there in the wind. You need the right support. By that, I mean a set of street-smart guidelines for dating, mating, and whatever comes before, after, and in between.

Sharing a house on the Shore with four fist-pumping Guidos gave me a unique perspective on the opposite sex. We were in seriously close quarters. Besides witnessing the GTL ritual in action, I got to listen to the guys giving their play-by-plays of the hookups from the night before (trust me, ladies—it's not pretty). I got to experience them in their natural habitat—the clubs—creeping on chicks. I got to watch relationships build and crumble. I got to see people looking for love and people only looking for sex. I now understand much more about what makes men tick. Or at the very least, how to tick them off. It was eye-opening (although, occasionally nauseating!), and I thank my housemates for giving me an up-close and personal view of the male species. Even if it sometimes meant I saw a little more than I wanted . . .

But even if you're not a Guido/Guidette or into the whole club culture, I've discovered that there are several universal truths you can apply in any situation—and even with a guy like The Situation. My dating rules are about self-respect and strength and keeping your eyes open when you're in a relationship. It sounds simple, but when you're infatuated with a guy, all common sense tends to go out the window. You do things without considering the consequences. You take a lot of shit that you would normally never put up with. Sometimes you even lose yourself. So you need some basic principles to keep you grounded, to put things in perspective. These rules apply to anyone, no matter where you're from, no matter who you're with, be it a guy you just met at a bar or someone you've been dating for a year and you hope is your future fiancé. They'll even help you if you're single and on the prowl. You'll learn to weed out the losers and zone in on the men worthy of you. You'll be a man magnet, but only for the best guys because the scumbags will know you're onto them and keep their distance. You'll have the power, the knowledge, the walk and the talk, and the ability to put it all into motion.

Once you have my rules, you have to stick to them. No excuses, no exceptions. When I didn't follow them, my relationships wound up in the toilet. I found myself with the wrong guys, compromising who I was, and trying to justify sticking it out when walking away would have been a much smarter choice. I was miserable. I cried and bitched and moaned about the losers I was with. Then, suddenly, one day it hit me: enough is enough. No self-respecting woman deserves to be treated like some guy's dirty laundry. I wanted more. I was sick of settling. I was better than this. I needed a good slap in the face to set me straight.

Since none of my *Shore* mates volunteered for that job (I'd probably have kicked their asses if they tried), I gave myself my own wake-up call. I went back and dissected every relationship that failed: what I did/he did/we did. I was brutally honest. Suddenly the pieces began to fall into place. I could see all the red flags that were there that I hadn't noticed while I was living it. I could see the same patterns over and over.

That's how, in a nutshell, JWOWW's Rules were born. I made a list of everything I wanted in a relationship—what I wouldn't compromise on. Then I began to examine the types of guys I was dating and how they operated. Just in case no one has ever told you before, men are pretty transparent and predictable. And once you get what they're about, they're easy to manipulate. I live by these rules now and I'm a hell of a lot happier. I don't get used or abused. I even found love at the Jersey Shore, which is not something I ever expected or thought possible. My roommates love the guy I am seeing now. They see how much I smile and laugh. They never noticed this side of me before because I was so depressed and defensive. If we were playing Mike's little "Most Likely" game, I would have been "Most Likely to Start a Smackdown." But I swear, it's like a big dark cloud has lifted.

I feel like I have seen it all, heard it all, and done (just about) it all. Nothing scares me anymore (okay, maybe those disgusting deep-fried frog legs from Miami, but that's about it . . .). I have experienced more in my twenty-five years than most women twice my age. And I screwed up. Big-time. Several of my relationships have been train wrecks. I don't think it's always a good thing to smush and tell . . . but I figured that sharing these relationship horror stories might prevent other women from falling into the same traps I did.

We all have our horror stories and we all make mistakes. I have never come across a girl that got it right the first time—myself included. The trick is to learn from your mistakes. I'm badder and wiser now. I know you don't have to be stuck in a relationship that isn't working. You don't have to put up with bullshit or act like a fool. And most important, you don't have to hide who you really are just to make a guy like you. Any asshole who asks you to be someone you're not is not worthy of your backwash.

Maybe my guidelines are a little Guidette-harsh. I'll give you that; I call 'em like I see 'em, and sometimes my advice is in-your-face. The truth hurts. I am not gonna sugarcoat it, and you'll thank me later. Why? Because a guy won't be able to break your heart again when you see it coming a mile away. Because bitches will back off and steer clear of your man. Because you'll call the shots and learn how to get what (and who) you want in life. My *Shore* mates love this about me. In my house, I'm not just the hot one; I'm the big sister (with the big boobs). The one everyone feels comfortable coming to for advice. The boys, the girls—they know they can open up to me and I will be honest.

The Rules According to JWOWW is for the woman who wants to feel empowered; for the single girl tired of sitting home alone on a Saturday night; for every woman who's ever been dumped or lied to and is done with being a doormat. My rules will protect you in the long run. Follow them, and you'll be in control of your mind, your body, your actions. If the relationship goes south, then it'll be your partner who fucked it up, not you. There's no gray area where you're questioning "What did I do wrong?" or "Is there anything I could have done differently?" You'll never again be doubting or blaming yourself. You'll never again wonder if he's The One or merely a one-way ticket to hell. You'll know, and you'll know how to handle it, whether it means getting him to commit or getting his ass off your couch permanently.

But my rules aren't just mental. I'll be honest with you: looks matter. You do not want to be the grenade in your group. You want to look your freshest from head to toe, and that means body, skin, hair, and everything you wear. Total package. You want the inside and outside to be in sync. Which is why I have also included several rules on how to get in shape, eat right, dress, and do your hair and makeup. Believe me, guys notice if you make the effort, and it's another key manipulating tool.

So now the question is, are you ready? Are you ready to play by JWOWW's Rules and change the way you see men and the way they see you? Are you ready to be fierce, flirty, and play dirty if necessary?

If so, read on . . .

SHORE-SPEAK

GTL. DTF. Grenades, Gorillas, Juiceheads.
If you want to understand my rules, you gotta
learn to speak the language first!

BATTLE (VERB)

To wage a fun, competitive showdown on the dance floor—no violence necessary. Usually aimed at getting some hot girl's attention. As in, "Ronnie and Sitch were battling it out at Karma."

BLOWOUT (NOUN)

A Guido's fave hairstyle. For guys, it means coating hair with buckets of gel then using a dryer to blow it straight up into spikes. Pauly D perfected this look; according to him, it's "windproof, waterproof, soccer-proof, motorcycle-proof. Possibly bulletproof as well." When a girl does a blowout, it's to straighten and volumize her hair. See chapter 8 for how-tos.

BOO-BOO (NOUN)

A sweet little nickname me and Nicole (aka Snooki) call each other.

BUSINESS, THE (NOUN)

Sex. The goal of every night for some Guidos. "Forget about eating. I wanna get to The Business."

BUSTED (ADJECTIVE)

Ugly. Your face looks like someone busted it up! A nasty-ass way to describe a girl. As in, "That girl is so busted. I'm embarrassed for the guy who brings her home tonight!"

CREEP (VERB)

To hit on girls. Basically, to go out and pick up women with the sole intention of getting laid. As in, "Hey, dude. Let's go creep tonight!"

DTS/DTF (ADJECTIVE)

Down to smush/down to fuck. A way to describe a girl or guy who's looking to get laid and doesn't need any persuading. Common way to ask: "You DTF?"

FRESH TO DEATH (ADJECTIVE)

What both men and women say to each other when we look amazing; when we're sporting new clothes, good hair, great tan, a nice manicure, etc. Synonym: mint.

FIST PUMP (NOUN/VERB)

The telltale sign of a Guido on the dance floor. They punch the air with one hand, usually in groups, to house music—normally during the part where the beat is building.

FROLIC (NOUN/VERB)

The female version of a fist pump.

GORILLA (NOUN)

A guy with huge, ripped muscles. Usually between the ages of twenty-one and thirty-eight.

MONKEY (NOUN)

A gorilla who's under twenty-one.

APE (NOUN)

A gorilla who's over thirty-eight.

SILVER-BACK (NOUN)

An old gorilla—like Arnold Schwarzenegger or Vinny's Nino.

GRENADE (NOUN)

A large, ugly chick who's friends with a hot chick. As in, "Just in case a grenade gets thrown at you, one of your buddies takes it first . . ." Can also mean a friend who protects her pal from being hit on. As in, "I was trying to make my move, and this grenade comes out of nowhere and blocks me."

LAND MINE (NOUN)

A thin grenade.

GRENADE LAUNCHER (NOUN)

A bigger and stronger grenade. She can kick your ass.

GRUNDEL OR CHOAD (NOUN)

Male versions of a grenade or land mine.

GFA/GFF

Grenade-free America/Grenade-free foundation. What the guys vowed to keep our Miami pad, but of course, never followed through on since they all hooked up with an ugly chick at least once.

THE GIRLS (NOUN)

Boobs, tits, cleavage—your pair. As in, "I love that sling-back shirt—it really shows off The Girls."

GTL (PHRASE)

A Guido's daily ritual: gym, tanning, laundry. They believe it is the key to a put-together, ready-to-creep Guido. As in, "If you want to look mint, you gotta GTL."

GRIND (VERB)

Dancing with someone in a sexual manner; grinding your bodies together. In essence, dancing crotch to crotch as opposed to cheek to cheek.

HATER (NOUN)

Someone who disapproves of what you're doing—or is jealous of what you're doing and is pretty vocal about it. As in, "Why are you being such a hater? Why don't you mind your own business?" Can also be used as a verb: "Why are you hating on me?"

JUICEHEAD (NOUN)

A big, muscular guy who does steroids or works out so much that he looks like he does steroids.

JUICE BAD (NOUN)

A juicehead with an attitude.

INTRODUCTION

JUST SAYIN' (PHRASE)
What me and Snooks say to each other after we say
something funny—or to make fun of something.
Example: "That bag doesn't say Gucci, it says Poochi.
Just sayin'!"

LEAN CUISINE (NOUN)
A good-looking guy who's in shape but thin.

MVP (NOUN)
The holy trio: Mike, Vinny, and Pauly.

NAPOLEON (NOUN)
A guy who's too short to date.

ONE-NIGHTER (NOUN)
Aka, hit it and quit it! A person who is solely in it for the
sex, who wants to be a one-night stand and nothing more.

POUF (NOUN)
The hairstyle Nicole made famous, which is now the
sign of a true Guidette everywhere (since everyone
wants to be Snooks!). She's been wearing it since she
was sixteen. To do it, tease up a large portion of hair at
the crown into a pouf, and secure with a banana clip.

POUND (VERB)
To have aggressive sex; also to knock back a lot of

alcohol. Examples: "He was really pounding me last night . . . I'm walkin' funny!" or "Jeez, she was really pounding back the Ron-Ron juice."

ROBBERY (NOUN)

To steal a girl some other guy was just hitting on. As in, "When Vinny went to the men's room at Karma, Sitch pulled a robbery on him."

RON–RON JUICE (NOUN)

Ronnie's lethal precreeping cocktail. He says it's the root of all evil. Basically, a blend of watermelon, cherries, cranberry juice, vodka, and ice.

SITUATION (NOUN)

Aside from Mike's self-declared nickname (since he likes to flaunt his), it means well-defined, six-pack abs.

SMUSH (VERB)

To have sex. Ideally with a Guido or Guidette.

STAGE 5 CLINGER (NOUN)

A girl or guy who becomes overly attached and clingy early on in the relationship. He/she calls, texts, demands seeing you every night, etc. Also, Stage 5 stalker.

TYPICAL JERK–OFF (NOUN)

A guy that's a textbook asshole. Also known as a dirtbag, douchebag, scumbag. Or a combo of all the above.

VIBE (VERB)

To be into someone, attracted to them. As in, "Me and Joey, we're vibin'."

WIFE-UP (VERB)

To treat a woman as if she is a potential girlfriend/wife. This may include wining, dining, buying her gifts, treating her with respect. The girl has to be seriously special for a guy to go to these lengths. For example, when Pauly met Rocio, he was ready to "wife-up." In Jersey, my boyfriend did the right things to wife-me-up.

WING MAN/WING WOMAN (NOUN)

A good friend who helps you hook up and watches out for your ass when you're too shit-faced to do so. Duties can include making introductions, keeping his/her friend occupied so a number exchange can happen, or taking a grenade for your Boo Boo.

ZOO CREATURE (NOUN)

Another way of calling someone a grenade launcher. This is a big, nasty girl who tends to get mean and physical when provoked (or you take her toys away). Also called a hippo or an elephant. The guys in the house have a talent for bringing these types back to our hot tub.

CHAPTER 2

ON THE PROWL

RULE 1: YOU GOTTA BE IN IT TO WIN IT

Just like the Jersey lottery. You can't sit around in your ratty sweats waiting for Prince Charming to come galloping up to your beach house. You have to hit the scene and go looking for him. Clubbing, barhopping, if you're twenty-one or older, even combing the beach or working out at the gym—there are men to be found everywhere. It's like a buffet at a big Italian wedding. So why the hell can't you find one? Maybe because you're a woman who complains all the time yet doesn't take action. Sitting home, eating a pint of Ben & Jerry's, and watching Lifetime (or even better, *Jersey Shore*!) isn't going to get you a guy. You can't replace a man with mint chocolate chip.

I know for some women the face-to-face approach

is intimidating. They cringe at the idea of putting themselves "out there" because it means they're opening themselves up to the possibility of public rejection. You have to make peace with the fact that you are going to be scoped out and judged. I won't kid you—it takes balls to be in the scene. Look at me! Look at the clothes I wear! You don't think I'm judged? Hell yeah I am. The difference is, I embrace it and run with it. Judge all you want, baby! Everyone has been rejected at one time or another—some people more often than a telemarketer. Even the people in my house (who will remain nameless) who claim it has *never* happened to them. You can't fool me; I was there, dude. I saw the skid marks.

You should never let fear of rejection hold you back. It's a lame excuse; rejection won't kill you, it will only make you stronger. And you can't take it that personally: maybe it's not you. Maybe he's just a dick and you need to keep it moving. I used to be a mess when a guy broke up with me, but now I know better. I never think for a second that the world is going to end over this guy. And there's plenty more where he came from. For every dozen meatheads you meet out there, there are usually one or two decent guys that are worth getting to know. Those are about the odds. And the more you do it, the easier it gets and the better you get at it.

Besides, what other options do you have? Well, let's think about that: you could let your friends fix you up with a friend or relative. So that way, if it doesn't work out, you piss off both your girlfriend and her big bro and neither is talking to you. Or you could try to find your match online—because anyone halfway decent is gonna hide behind a keyboard and call himself "2Hot4U." I know a lot of people are into online dating and would disagree with me on this, but I think it should be a last resort. How easy is it for a guy to deceive you when you can't see his sorry lying ass? And how much can you tell from reading someone's inflated profile or cyber-chatting? Okay, maybe he gives good sextext—a lot of them do. But that's not a basis for a solid relationship.

I am a firm believer in real one-to-one personal contact—the kind that involves looking someone in the eye and making small talk. I want to snuggle up to a warm body. I need to feel that initial attraction when you brush against him on the dance floor or your eyes meet across the bar. That spark is exciting and intoxicating. That's chemistry, baby. You need to see how you connect physically and mentally when you're in the same room. All you get from sitting around scrolling websites for love is dimples in your ass.

RULE 2: MAKE SURE YOU HAVE SOME PROTECTION

By this, I don't mean carry a pack of Trojans in your purse (although it's a good idea to be prepared!). I mean take a girlfriend or two with you to the club. When you go into battle, you should always surround yourself with your strongest troops. They'll help you repel the losers and reel in the hotties. Snook is my best friend, and I would do anything for her. Most of the time it means protecting her from making a mistake clouded over by soco goggles. But other times, I have to take one for the team. It's a fact that a man will not be himself when he's surrounded by his posse. That's when you need to pull a distraction maneuver. You keep his friend busy while your girl gets her one-on-one time. If one of my girlfriends needs my help in this department, I give them the ten-minute rule: make something happen in ten minutes, most likely exchange numbers. That's how long I will entertain the friend. Once you do the number swap, I'm running for the bathroom to disinfect the nasty off me and continue my night!

RULE 3: WHEN YOU'RE LEAST LOOKING FOR IT, LOVE WILL BITE YOU IN THE ASS

It's like some sick dating irony; you stop looking under rocks for Mr. Right and suddenly he appears. I swear, guys can smell desperation. It's like wearing a sign around your neck that says MAKE ME YOUR BALL AND CHAIN! I'd run, too. And when you ditch that scent, they're drawn to you. You will always meet someone that's right for you when you least expect it. Of course, that means you have to stop obsessing and get your mind off finding The One. When you go out, make it just about having fun, cutting loose, enjoying the moment. Trust me: men will pick up on this vibe. You can man-hunt anywhere, and that's the key: you should be going everywhere and keeping busy. I love places like the gym, parks, clubs, lounges, the beach, and sports bars, especially when there are big games going on. I strongly suggest becoming a baseball or football fan or at least learning the difference between a home run and a touchdown so you can make conversation. A bar packed with rabid sports fans is a great captive audience—and besides, there's usually free beer and wings.

RULE 4: A BAD ATTITUDE WILL DRAW LOSERS TO YOU LIKE FLIES TO GARBAGE

I am all for a girl being a badass when she needs to be—I wrote the book on that. But walking into a club with a chip on your shoulder is like broadcasting to every dirt-bag in the room, "Come and get me!" Whatever energy you radiate will attract the same energy, and it will come hurtling back in your face. Confidence is one thing; out-of-control hater bitch with an ax to grind is another. I will not walk into a club feeling like shit because I know I will only attract shit. Sometimes, if I am having a bad day, I have to give myself a little pep talk before I hit the road. I might take a shot and say, "Tonight's gonna be a good night and I'm gonna chill with the hottest gorilla in the club!" Other times, I'll just skip going out and sleep it off. There's always tomorrow. Because trust me, you do not want to be drinking when you're miserable. Alcohol will only amplify that foul mood, and an angry drunk is just asking to wind up in cuffs on *Cops*.

Also, guys hate a Debbie Downer. It's the ultimate turnoff. They don't like to hear women complain. If you look good, they'll stand there and let you vent for a few minutes, but they're thinking, "If she bitches and whines now when I just met her, what will it be like a week down the road?" And just like that, you've lost them. So my advice to you is this: put on a happy face. Sometimes, just freshening up will help you shake off your irritability. Do your hair and makeup, put on your hottest outfit. Tell yourself you're going to have a good time and put any other possibility out of your head. It may sound like Mary Poppins bullshit to say "think positive," but I swear to you, it works.

Case in point: I'll never forget meeting my current boyfriend—let's just call him "Perfection"—a few years ago. I walked into the club with one of my classic slingback shirts, ripped jeans, and my hair and makeup done up. I felt hot. I felt on top of the world. And just then, we made eye contact. It was like we were both caught in some magnetic force field. Within minutes we were talking up a storm and having a blast. The positive energy is what drew us to each other and past all the other people in the club. We still talk about that night and the great vibe we had between us.

RULE 5: LEARN TO SPOT A MAN–WHORE A MILE AWAY

Or a Guido or a virgin for that matter. This is a necessity. It will save you time, energy, and aggravation. When you've been on the scene as much as I have, you get pretty good at sizing 'em up and picking 'em out. I don't need more than a quick glance to ID a cocky asshole. It's a talent.

Since I was a teenager, I've been going out. But I never played the hookup game or went any further than kissing (a good policy to follow if you're under twenty-one!) because I was already in my first relationship when I was seventeen. I was off the market—which probably made me even better at observing others in action. The first time I really experienced clubbing as a single lady was when I moved to Long Island in 2006. I was twenty-one and ready to take over the scene. This is also when I met my first Guidos. For me, it was love at first sight, but they didn't want to give me the time of day. I came from upstate N.Y. and I was a tomboy; I didn't fit the part of the Guidette. So I stepped up my game, broke all the barriers, and created my own style. I went out in a skintight dress with my boobs and ass looking amazing, and that's how I got noticed. It's also when all the girls in Long Island started talking shit about me; I was the new girl everyone was hating on. But that's a good thing because, if they're hating or talking about you, you're doing something right.

Every time I walked by the DJ booth, the MC always said "Wow!" on the mic. A few months later we met up and started working together at a club, and he gave me my stage name, Jenni WOWW (later shortened to JWOWW). So between working at clubs and prowling, I got quite an education.

If you're not yet a regular on the scene, this guide to guys you'll meet in a club will come in handy. Commit it to memory, and you'll be prepared when one of these types crosses your path:

THE MAN-WHORE

He's bouncing around the club, passing out his number to any willing taker (and some not so willing ones as well). For him, it's all about quantity, not quality. You know the type: he stocks up on jumbo-size boxes of condoms at Costco. He's already dated half the female population of the tristate area, including one or more of your friends. Walk away. Run if you have to. Even if he is unbelievably sexy with a body like Hercules, it ain't worth it. If there is one dating rule I hold sacred, it's this: if you have been with one of my friends, you are not getting in my pants. Put it like this: you get serious with this guy and you're still friends with this girl. Are you going to allow them both in the same room? Especially if she's seen his penis? Come on . . . get real. This is a lose-lose situation. You're either going to lose your friend because you're dating him, or lose both of them when you find them screwing again in your bed. Just sayin' . . .

THE GUIDO

Most likely, he is from the East Coast. You will either see him doing shots at the bar or fist-pumping on the dance floor. He'll probably have spiky hair, a tight shirt, lots of tattoos, and be very tan with big muscles. The Guido is a tricky breed of man. If you want to get to know him, the worst place is at the nightclub, because Guidos roll in packs and his boys will not permit him to talk to you for too long. He will have to act like a hard-ass in front of his friends. The best way to try to make something out of this is to approach with confidence. Talk to him for ten to fifteen minutes. Give him your number and/ or take his. If he calls you and wants to meet up, make sure he leaves his posse behind. A Guido will only truly let his guard down when his friends aren't there busting on him.

But another warning: Guido's are hard to lock down in a relationship. Very, very hard. It takes years of experience, which I finally have, but let me tell you: it's a roller coaster ride from hell. If you're up to the challenge, go for it (and see chapter 4 for how to get a man to commit). If not, remember they're nice to look at.

THE CHEATER

I can smell a cheater a mile away. Cocky, arrogant SOBs. They think they're too much man for just one woman to handle—so they spread themselves around like fertilizer on your lawn (and you know what that stuff's made of, right?). The cheater is always with a couple of guys who are nudging him as if he's cool or something; they're egging him on to cheat! He doesn't make it that obvious by calling you another girl's name (though, I wouldn't put it past him!), but there are signs, lots of signs. He's really pushy, aggressive, and expecting something out of you right away—it's almost too obvious that you're going to be a one-night stand. Or he's always looking over his shoulder and nervously glancing around. Maybe he even occasionally flips out if he sees one of his girlfriend's friends and tries to hide or make a run for the door. Another dead giveaway? He gets all defensive and sweaty or gives you some lame excuse when you ask what's up with the weird act. Take it from me: once a cheater, always a cheater. Even if you wind up dating him, he'll two-time you as well.

MR. SMOOTH

I like this type. It's the guy that's not overly dressed for the occasion. He has a nice swagger about him—he's very calm, cool, and collected. He's chivalrous: he opens doors, buys drinks, says please and thank you. Pays you compliments and asks and answers questions without sounding cocky or arrogant. You'll find he doesn't go into much depth about himself—so he leaves you wanting more. There is an air of mystery about him, but he's not doing it to screw with your head. He's just laid-back and wants to let you get to know him layer by layer, inch by inch . . .

THE COCKY ASSHOLE

We all fall for this type once or twice. No matter how full of himself he is, you can't help being attracted. He has a magnetic pull on the opposite sex. I personally think it's the attitude. Confidence is seductive. He thinks he's a catch, so of course you think so, too. This type is often a bragging blowhard who throws around his cash like he owns the world. Sexy? Hell yeah. And there's something thrilling about how he bitches people out and belittles them. He just projects power. But I'll let you in on a little secret: beneath all that bravado, there's probably a ton of insecurity. Get him in bed, and chances are he'll be a "little" disappointing, if you get my drift. Sad but true.

THE VIRGIN

Before you skip this section or fall on the floor laughing, let me tell you these guys are *fun*. If you're a dominant woman that wants full control in a relationship, then a virgin is your dream guy. If you end up popping this guy's cherry, you are golden. He will be your little puppy dog that you can manipulate any way you want. That, of course, is the best-case scenario. He might have some weird problem (like a mommy complex) that you want to avoid. But let's be optimistic, shall we? The virgin is very easy to seek out at a club. He's usually horribly shy and nursing a drink somewhere in a dark, secluded corner. You're going to have to approach him, make conversation, put him at his ease. Be gentle. Once you break him in, he'll be an insatiable tiger in bed—with no bad habits to break.

THE NERD

He's not my type (I'm a Guidette and I need a Guido, a man's man!) but he might be yours. He may look clueless, but can often have a bit of an attitude about his intelligence. Then you've got a cocky brainiac on your hands. But most of the time, a nerd is quiet, shy, awkward, and a fairly easy catch if you're a somewhat attractive woman. Maybe you're drawn to his brain, not his bod. Just keep this in mind: are you compatible? I for one can't be with a guy who crunches numbers for a living while I'm taking shots and frolicking on the dance floor. But hey, if you can, more power to ya!

THE DRUNK

The most annoying guy at the club. I can't stand the loud, intoxicated, sweaty guy that is all over you and breathing down your neck. When he talks to you, he has that wasted glaze in his eyes. This type is very rude, too. I've heard it all. Either he'll start crying about how his dad never loved him or he'll make a comment about how fat your ass looks in that dress. What's in their heads is out of their mouths—which incidentally stink of booze (Altoid anyone?). Be cautious. Cute as he may be, nothing long-term comes out of a relationship with this dude—except maybe Twelve Steps.

RULE 6: REMEMBER THAT A GUY WILL SAY ANYTHING TO GET IN YOUR PANTS

There is not a line I haven't heard. Even the most original ones are variations on a theme. To break the ice in a loud, crowded space, a man will creep up to you and spring one of these openers. I swear, they must hand out a list when a guy hits puberty: Lame Things to Say to Girls. What ever happened to "Hey, my name is Joey. Nice to meet ya"? No, they have to be slicker than that. They have to actually get in your face and announce, "Someone call 911, 'cause I am the bomb!" Some even accompany their catchphrase with a visual—like exposing one's six-pack "situation" for example. But no matter what pickup lines they come up with, they all fall into a few categories:

FLATTERING

The guy who tries this line figures if he kisses your ass, you'll put out, i.e.: "You must have the wrong place. The beauty pageant is next door."

SMOOTH

Casanova thinks he is so cool and clever. He tries to talk a good game. Too bad his attempt at conversation makes you want to hurl. For example, "Could you please catch me? 'Cause I just fell for you!" Lame, lame, lame.

BRAGGING

Why do men think that acting like an egotistical douche-bag will win them women? Would you really give a guy your number if he said, "Just rub my lamp, baby, and I'll make all your dreams come true!"

JOKING

Maybe a fellow Guido would find this sort of thing funny, but no girl would go for it. Example: "Did you just fart? 'Cause you blew me away!" Keep moving, dude . . .

RULE 7: NOT ALL CLUBS ARE CREATED EQUAL

I recommend doing a little research before you decide to hit one you've never been to. Who hangs there? How hard is it to get in? Will you fit in or stand out? Do people go there to meet people . . . or just to be seen? Ask around. Where do your friends and their friends go? How about the people you work with—where do they go after hours to blow off steam? Thanks to *Jersey Shore*, I got to sample both Jersey and Miami clubs—they're two different worlds.

Jersey clubs remind me of college. They're all about partying and getting drunk, hooking up and having a good time. Everyone starts out looking hot as hell, and at the end of the night, you're a sweaty mess from dancing and working the crowd (and God knows what else went on in some secluded corner). Jersey clubs are home to me because they really get the party started.

Miami clubs are more for people wanting to be seen. It's the martini look. They do a lot of bottle service and it's always a dick contest to see who spends the most on bottles. All the guys invite the hottest girls into the VIP to make themselves look good. It's more like a late-night social hour than a party on the dance floor. To each his own. Miami does have some pretty insane clubs, but there's not enough for me to move down there. But I will say this: Miami holds my favorite conference of the year. It's the Winter Music Conference, aka Guido Central.

House DJs from all over the world flock down there for one week in March and with them follows every Guido, gearing up to fist-pump his heart out. True insanity.

JWOWW'S FAVE CLUBS

....

Hit these spots and you might see me hitting the dance floor!

IN MIAMI . . .
Space
Nocturnal
Mansion
Nikki Beach
Tantra
Bed

ON THE JERSEY SHORE . . .
Karma
Bamboo
Beachcomber
Aztec

MY HOME, LONG ISLAND . . .
Glo
Neptune Beach Club
Savannah

RULE 8: SLOPPY DRUNK IS NOT A GOOD LOOK ON ANYONE

Okay, I'm all for getting a buzz on. It's a nice way to help you kick back, relax, let your guard down. But shit-faced is a whole other story. There is just no need and nothing good can come of it. You will most likely do something—or somebody—that you'll regret in the A.M. I made a bad call one of the first nights at the *Shore* house when I hooked up with Pauly. Even though he's great-looking and I was attracted to him, I knew it was going to go nowhere and I was still in a relationship. Also, Pauly and I are great friends now, so it's sometimes hard to look past the fact that one of our first nights of getting to know each other we made out and I saw his penis! Drinking too much can also lower your standards when it comes to men. Trust me; you don't want to wake up next to a hippo because you had one too many SoCos.

So my advice to you is this: be smart when you drink (and don't drink if you're underage!) Always have your backup—your girlfriends—there to make sure you get home in one piece sans a scumbag hanging all over you. Tell your girls they have the right to stage an intervention if you're out of control; a citizen's arrest if they have to. A few other drinking rules to follow:

DRINK WHAT YOU KNOW

If you've never tried a Suck, Bang, and Blow, I do not recommend sampling this drink—or any other strange new
one—when you're out prowling. Don't order the bar's
specialty cocktail just because it sounds cool—you never
know what the hell is in it. Something can taste fruity and
weak but knock you off your ass twenty minutes later.
Stick to what you know you can tolerate. For me, that's
vodka seltzers. I drink them if I just want to have a light
buzz but still be on point. The seltzer lightens up the alcohol, so it doesn't go straight to my head. On the flip side, I
know if I start with a Long Island iced tea, I will be drunk
as a skunk in no time. I also try to avoid taking shots
because I don't want to get too sloppy, too fast. They may
come in tiny little glasses but they pack a mighty punch.

SKIP THE SUGARY DRINKS

Besides being high in calories, they mask the taste of
the alcohol, so you tend to drink more without realiz-
ing how much you're actually consuming. And they also
cause hangovers.

STAY HYDRATED

Alcohol dries your body out faster than laying out on the
beach. Drink water, soda, or fitness water in between
every glass of booze you down. Drinking a one-to-one

ratio of nonalcoholic and alcoholic beverages is a good policy; that's one glass of water or Diet Coke for every serving of alcohol.

PACE YOURSELF

You may feel fine after the first two margaritas, but don't jump right into a third. It might take your body and your brain a while to feel the effects. Drink slowly. It's not a contest to see who can hurl first.

DON'T DRINK ON AN EMPTY STOMACH

Guaranteed, you'll get wasted, or worse, puke your guts out. Eat before you go out and during as well if you're planning on a long night. Right before I go out, I make sure I grab a granola bar and a large glass of water. It's filling and it will hydrate you for the long night ahead. In a pinch, know those pretzels they serve on the bar? Grab a handful: they soak up the alcohol pretty well.

STOP DRINKING IF YOU FEEL OUT OF CONTROL

Slurred speech, blurry vision, trouble walking or remembering your own name. Stop! One of my worst drinking experiences was when I was in Atlantic City with my roommates. I started off with champagne when we got to the hotel, then at dinner I had some wine. Before I knew it, we were at the club drinking shots and chugging back vodka cranberries. I mixed every alcohol known to a bar that night, and I was a complete wreck. I hurled then I got all pissed, and later I punched Mike in the face back at the room. What a night! I learned my lesson not to ever do that again.

STOP DRINKING IF YOU VOMIT

If you puke it up, don't put more in. Vomiting is a signal that your body can't take the amount of alcohol that you have consumed. Call it quits for the evening and go clean yourself up at home.

DESIGNATE A DRIVER

This goes without saying if you're driving to a club. Or arrange for cab service like we did in Miami. There is no way you or anyone in your posse who has been drinking should get behind a wheel. I don't care how few drinks you had or how long you've had to run them down. *Never.*

RULE 9: IT'S OKAY FOR A WOMAN TO MAKE THE FIRST MOVE

I am all about women being the aggressor. It feels empowering to me to be able to strut over to a guy, tell him he's cute, and give him my number. If he calls me, great. If he doesn't, his loss. That's how you have to look at this.

Some guys will be totally turned on by a woman who sees what she likes and goes after it. Others—usually the ones with the biggest egos and smallest brains and other body parts—prefer to do the creeping. Whatever. But don't let that hold you back. Nothing ventured, nothing gained. You don't have to pounce on the guy—just sneak up next to him on the dance floor or walk over to where he's standing and say, "Hi." Ask him about himself. Guys LOVE to talk about themselves; most will do it all night if they have a captive audience. What are his hobbies? Where does he live? Where does he work? How did he get so hot . . . you get the idea. You may have to endure a long monologue about how awesome he is. But if in the end you get a date out of it . . . totally worth being bored to tears, don't you think? Even though she likes to joke around, Snooks is pretty straightforward when it comes to approaching a guy. If she's attracted, she'll waste no time in the small-talk department and see where it ends up by the end of the night. That's my girl!

Here are a few no-pressure openers that will get the conversation going:

- "Do you come here a lot?"
- "This music is great, don't you think?"
- "What are you drinking?"
- "Are you from around here?"
- "You look really familiar . . ."
- "Hi." (Basically, that's about all a guy needs to hear to get his attention.)

BITCHES YOU MIGHT MEET ON THE SCENE

....

Oh, yeah, they're everywhere. Try to keep away because these broads make the Wicked Witch look like Mother Teresa.

THE MARRIAGE WRECKER

This type of woman knows a guy is married and doesn't give a fuck. In fact, it turns her on. Stealing another woman's man is a power play. This bitch is one of the worst in my book. I have even seen them go to the extreme of hooking up only with married guys because they have a certain agenda (i.e., take pics of the night and use it against the guy to get money out of them so they won't tell their wives). Truly disgusting. But I look at it like this: if the guy is willing to cheat, he deserves whatever he's got coming to him. Both of them are trash in my book.

THE HIPPO

A heavyset woman at the club who likes to throw her weight around and behave like a zoo animal. Look, I don't discriminate against anyone who's willing to have a good time at the club. You should be comfortable in your own skin and do your thing, no matter what size you are. But these are not just big women; they're women with a big attitude. They like to get pushy and pick fights, and they think they can scare off smaller girls who are afraid of getting their asses kicked. Remember the bitches that came calling at our house for Sitch? Poor Snooks tried to step in and save her housemate and an animal came at her, swinging. This is the kind of behavior I am talking about. Inexcusable. But I am not afraid of this type of beast. Bring it on. I can take you with my eyes closed.

THE EXTREME FAKER

There's a fine art to fakin' it. I have no issues with women (like me) who heighten their attributes with breast augmentation, hair extensions, and nails. If it makes you feel good about yourself, go for it. What I am talking about here, though, is the type of woman—mostly found in the tristate area—who has gone overboard enhancing every inch of herself. Who considers plastic surgery a pastime. These women go to clubs and act like their shit don't stink. They're fake head to toe: overtanned, dragon-lady nails, collagen lips, Botox, makeup like a clown, and hair that is so Aqua Netted it can't move and might catch on fire if someone lights a match. The clothes are too tight, the handbag is a knockoff, and they're busy snapping their gum and eyeing up all the girls in the club like everyone is beneath them. These women have severe insecurity issues, so I don't even sweat them. They are out six nights a week, preying on guys and posting their pictures ("Don't I look hot?") on Facebook. Pathetic.

THE DRAMA QUEEN

She's just itchin' for a fight—everything you say and do sets this one off. Bump into her, look at her the wrong way, accidentally spill your drink on her, even fucking sneeze in her direction, and she's suddenly in your face, mouthing off and bitching that you did her wrong. What she wants is to get a rise out of you—she lives for drama because she's insecure and wants to be the center of attention. She's the classic schoolyard bully—only more fucked up. So if you ignore her, if you just walk away from her tirade and resist the urge to give her the finger or rip her hair out (tempting as that is), she'll be forced to take it down a notch since no one is paying attention. You'll find a lot of this type lurking around the clubs—a drama queen loves a standing-room-only audience. Just be thankful you don't have one living in your Shore house!

RULE 10: BODY LANGUAGE SPEAKS
LOUDER THAN WORDS

If you want to let a guy know you're vibing on him, why not drop a few signals? Lick your lips, twirl your hair, suck on a straw (he'll get the picture from that one, I promise you). This is a great pickup technique for women who are too shy/nervous to strike up a conversation. Let your body do the talking for you. Think of it as another fun way to flirt—without the pressure of making small talk.

FIVE SIGNS THAT SAY "I'M HOT FOR YOU"

1. **Raise your brows**. When you catch a guy's gaze across the bar, smile, then raise both eyebrows in a quick flash, then lower them. Body-language experts say this indicates excitement and arousal. I think it says, "Yeah, you know what I'm thinking . . ."

2. **Lean in.** Especially effective if you're sporting serious cleavage, like I try to do. The first night I met Perfection, I had my sling-back shirt on and used it to my full advantage while I bent forward to give him a gander of The Girls. When he's talking, bend from the waist in his direction. Just watch where his eyes are drawn! It's a move that not only calls attention to your

boobs but says, "I am into you." If he returns the action and leans into you . . . score!

3. **Lick your lips**. It's a direct sign of sexual interest—no shitting. As is a lip pucker (like you're ready for a kiss), or you could even trace your lips with your pointer finger in a slow, seductive way. Basically, anything you do with your mouth is going to make a guy think of sex. It's a no-brainer.

4. **Twirl your hair**. As you give him "the look," slowly wind a few strands of hair seductively around your fingers. Or run your fingertips through your hair, then give it a toss. Sammi has perfected the hair touch move. Guys will often do this move, too. Watch for a guy who strokes his beard or mustache or runs his hands through the spikes in his hair. He's telling you he wants you.

5. **Cross your legs**. Do not try this move if you're going Britney-commando for the night. There better be some sexy underwear under there and, it goes without saying . . . a wax job. When you're seated with a guy on a couch in a lounge or at a bar stool, cross your legs, then cross them the other way. He won't see much; maybe just a quick glimpse of red lace. But experts say this communicates a subtle, sexual invitation: "Come and get it, Guido . . ."

FIVE SIGNS THAT SAY "I'M NOT INTERESTED"

Occasionally, you may want to use body language to communicate the opposite of the above: as in, "Back off, loser. Peddle your wares elsewhere . . ." These signals say it all without you having to get mean in his face or hurt anyone's feelings.

1. **Look away**. If your eyes meet—and you have no interest—then break eye contact. It says you're bored, bothered, or about to blow him off. There's nothing subtle about it—you can't bear to look at his mug for one more second.

2. **Cross your hands in your lap**. It screams, "Sorry, buddy, I'm not open for Business." Another variation: arms crossed over your breasts. Hands off!

3. **Pull away**. The opposite of the lean in. If he goes forward and you go back—kind of like a seesaw—then you're saying you're not into him and you prefer that he keep his distance.

4. **Yawn.** Don't attempt to stifle it—yawn right in his face so he sees he's boring the shit out of you.

5. **Wrinkle your nose** . . . like you're disgusted. Like he stinks. He'll think he has BO and make a beeline for

the door. Rolling your eyes is also a good gesture that shows that you either think he's an idiot or you could care less what he's saying. If none of these work, do what I do. Say "I'm not interested, so please back the fuck off."

COCKTAILS, ANYONE?

....

Jersey Shore–inspired, JWOWW approved. I used to bartend, so fair warning: my drinks are pretty lethal. It goes without saying (but I will say it anyway), do not try these if you are under twenty-one and never drink and drive!

LONG ISLAND ICED TEA

½ ounce vodka	½ ounce tequila (optional)
½ ounce gin	½ ounce triple sec
½ ounce rum	1 ounce sweet & sour

Fill a glass with ice. Add the vodka, gin, rum, tequila, if using, triple sec, and sweet & sour. Top with Coke. Garnish with a lemon twist.

SEX ON THE BEACH

1 ounce vodka
1 ounce peach schnapps

Orange juice
½ ounce melon liqueur

Fill a glass with ice. Add vodka and peach schnapps. Top with orange juice. Float melon liqueur on top. Garnish with a cherry.

ISLAND COOLER

½ ounce white rum
3 ounces pineapple juice

3 ounces quava juice
½ ounce dark rum

Fill a glass with ice. Add white rum and the juices to a shaker with ice. Shake well and strain into the glass. Float the dark rum on top. Garnish with a pineapple wedge.

LEMON-DROP MARTINI/SHOT

This is my specialty shot at the bar!
Smooth and nice, but warning: they get you banged up.

1 teaspoon sugar
1 tablespoon lemon juice
2 ounces vodka

1 ounce triple sec
2 ounces margarita mix

Place the sugar and lemon juice in a cocktail shaker. Swirl the shaker around so that both ingredients are mixed thoroughly. Add ice cubes. Add the vodka, triple sec, and margarita mix, and shake well. Strain into a cocktail glass.

RULE 11: DO NOT GO HOME
WITH A GUY YOU JUST MET

Unless you're just trying to get it in! My girl Snooks on occasion likes to bring home a guy to make out with, and there is nothing wrong with that. To each his own; I don't judge. My advice is strictly for dating and relationships, not hooking up. I never go home with a guy I just ran into at a club, and if you're not looking for a one-nighter, I strongly suggest you adopt the same hard-and-fast rule. You do not know this guy from a hole in the wall, and you never know his intentions. I always say play it safe. If he doesn't like it, tough shit. If he's really into you, he'll call you and you'll go out again and get to know each other better.

You will not make a guy like you by going home with him and hooking up. I had a conversation with my boyfriend the other day. I asked him if I went home with him our first night, would we be where we are now? He said probably not. Getting to know me, and getting me to like him enough to sleep with him, was the thrill. "It's like hunting," he said. "You travel for a day or two just to get to the location. Then you get up early and wait all day or even days to get the perfect deer. But if you walk out on your porch and shoot a deer and go back to bed, what the hell is the point? There's no thrill there. No excitement. No game."

Guys love what they can't have, and my man loved

that about me. He wanted the cat-and-mouse chase and the excitement that comes with the unknown. If you give it up the first night, you leave nothing to the imagination. And I guarantee that guy that pounded you out will not see you as girlfriend material from that point on. Why? Because if you do it with him, you can do it with anyone.

Here's the thing: guys appreciate a challenge. So every time you say no, it's like pouring gasoline on the fire. It will drive him wild, and he'll be even more determined to get you back in his bed. He will say anything to get you to come back with him. Don't cave in, even if he whines, begs, or assures you he's a perfect gentleman.

WHAT A GUY WILL SAY TO GET YOU IN THE SACK

....

You've gotta hand it to them for creativity and persistence. A+ for effort, but I'm not buying (and you shouldn't either) if you hear:

- "Let's just go back and hang out!"
- "I have a really cool hot tub . . ."
- "I'm starved . . . let's go back to my place and order a pizza."

- "My roommates are all gonna be there. We won't be alone . . ."
- "There's a really great movie on TV . . ."
- "I just wanna snuggle with you . . ."
- "Nothing will happen."

Do not believe for one second that "nothing will happen." Of course something will happen. You're asking for it by entering his "lair," aren't you? What if he's too drunk to stop himself? What if you're too drunk to say no? Too many what-ifs for my taste. If you have to, make up some excuse: "I'm really sorry, but I promised my roommate we'd meet up at two A.M. She doesn't have her keys . . ."

Trust me, I live with four Guido roommates, and let me tell you, nothing good ever comes from hooking up too soon except the funny stories the next day. It is a hard-and-fast rule that a Guido will never wife-up a one-nighter. He's a hit-it-and-quit-it kind of guy. Guidos do not respect these girls. In fact, they pat themselves on the back for scoring and see these women as just a piece of ass, a conquest. If that's what you want to be . . . be my guest. But I have way too much respect for myself.

PLAY IT SAFE

....

You may be leaving the club or bar very late at night—and often you're not familiar with the hood. If you are not with the group you came with, be careful and be smart.

- Make sure you always park close to the nightclub or have security bring you to your car if you're going home alone. But never drive to a club if you plan on drinking.

- If you didn't drive, make sure that when you hail a cab, it's in a spot where people can see you.

- Never go down grimy-looking side streets. Someone nasty might be lurking there.

- Just use your instincts. A woman's intuition is always right. So if something doesn't feel right, go with your gut feeling and avoid a bad situation.

RULE 12: NEVER LEAVE HOME WITHOUT THESE

I always carry these things in my purse when I'm out and about:

- Condoms. Necessary even if you're not expecting to go home with someone. You should always have a few handy, just in case.

- Cell phone. You need it to take down numbers, call or text a friend to come and get you if you're drunk and can't drive, etc.

- Cash and credit cards. You never want to rely on a guy to pay, and you want to show a guy you can pay for yourself or him. It's always good (and a classy move) to buy him a drink if he bought you one first. And I always make sure to have my "emergency $20 bill." Ya never know.

- Hair accessories such as comb, ponytail holder.

- Change of panties . . . hey, they could come in handy.

- Makeup. You always want your face to stay fresh. I always carry lip gloss, bronzer, blush brush, eyeliner.

- House keys/car keys.

RULE 13: HANGOVERS SUCK ... BUT ARE CURABLE

You overdid it and now your head feels like fifty Guidos are inside it doing the fist pump. You want to puke, you want to scream. Even your eyelashes hurt. Not to worry; JWOWW is the expert (thanks to much experience in this department) on curing hangovers fast. Pauly probably runs a close second.

Hangovers are better known as withdrawals from sugar with some dehydration mixed in for added torture. Basically, the more you drank the night before, the worse off you feel today. It's payback, I swear, for a great night of partying . . .

Flood yourself with fluids. I suggest a ton of water or Gatorade with two Tylenol or some sort of headache reliever.

Sleep—for at least eight hours. Your body needs the rest to replenish and recover. Most of us at the Shore house will sleep in till noon if we need to.

Avoid caffeine. A cup of coffee probably sounds good right now, but the caffeine will continue to dehydrate you. Instead, try a glass of fruit juice, which has vitamins.

Eat mineral-rich food like pickles (Snook's fave). Some people believe drinking pickle juice is a hangover remedy! You can also munch on whole wheat toast and cereal.

Take a shower, switching between cold and hot water. It will wake you up and ease the muscle aches.

Sweat it out at the gym. Exercise gets the blood pumping and helps the body release toxins.

Dear JWOWW:

I got totally wasted last night and woke up in my roommate's bed. I have no idea what happened, and I am friends with the dude. What should I do?

As I mentioned, too much alcohol is a one-way ticket to the walk of shame. Most of my *Shore* mates and I are guilty of getting a little too "friendly" with someone in the house after a wild night. Let's see: there was me and Pauly, Snooks and Vinny. . . . You get what I'm saying? It happens. It's not the end of the world or a reason to move out. Yeah, you're probably embarrassed as all shit, but just let it go. If he doesn't bring it up, then you don't bring it up. Maybe he has no fucking idea what happened either. If you don't see any evidence (condom wrapper on the floor, messy sheets, your panties hangin' on his head), then assume you were just getting cozy and passed out. You can still be friends even if you had one night of fringe benefits. If you do decide to discuss it, then keep it cool and casual—like it was no big deal, unless you want it to be one.

CHAPTER 3

DATING

RULE 14: LOVE IS A FREAKIN'
BATTLEFIELD—BE PREPARED

P at Benatar knew what she was talking about: you need a bulletproof vest if you're going to put your heart out there. Why? Because relationships can be brutal. I know this firsthand. For every good guy out there, there are dozens of douchebags that lie and cheat and then brag about it to their friends. Clubs are crawling with these serial scumbags. I know we all want to believe that true love is honest and beautiful and easy—the shit that they write about in Hallmark cards. But not in the circles I travel in and not in reality. So you have to be prepared and you have to be smart. I sure as shit wasn't.

As I warned you before, my early love life could easily pass for a horror flick. A few years ago, when I was naive and new to New York, I had a knack for landing losers. I like to think that my first relationship from hell—and all the lousy ones that followed—made me a stronger, wiser person. I took a beating (emotionally and even physically), but as a result, I grew balls. No one is going to pull that crap on me now. Not unless they have a death wish.

Let's call my first big mistake "The Guido." This was by far the most self-destructive relationship I have ever been in, so it's worth telling the nasty tale. I repeatedly let myself be this guy's emotional punching bag. He lied over and over again and I lapped it up like his puppy dog. When I moved to New York, I just wanted to have a good time. I ended up meeting this guy. He was tall, dark, and handsome with ridiculous features and even more ridiculous muscles. He was sexy and smart as hell, and he was deep into the club scene, which I wanted to explore. No one else would give me the time of day in New York, but he did. So, of course, I was in love. I was young and stupid and I wanted that crazy rush of the fast life. He had it all—even the sick BMW. Nothing like rolling in Long Island with the hottest guy in the hottest car. I thought I had scored big-time.

But nothing that looks this good on the outside is ever as good on the inside. The guy had major issues, and as we spent more time together, they began to slip through the cracks. Thanksgiving of '06 he asked me to pick him up at an after-hours club in NYC because he was too banged up to get home. Of course I came running; I was infatuated. I even drove through the fucking Macy's Thankgiving Day Parade traffic to rescue him.

After I picked him up and took him back to my house, he threw up several times. So much for romance. Then he showered and invited me back to his mother's for dinner. Okay, I thought, it's a step in the right direction. He's introducing me to the family. But as we were driving to his mother's house, he pulled over to the side of the road and dropped a bomb on me. I had visited his one-bedroom basement apartment many times before this and he told me it was all he could afford because living in Long Island is so expensive. I believed him. What I didn't know was that Mama was living upstairs! He always snuck me in the side entrance at night and claimed it was his own apartment. Total bullshit; it was his mother's place, and he didn't pay a cent of rent. Lie number one.

I was stunned, but I sucked it up and said it was okay—which it wasn't. What the fuck? I thought I was dating a mature guy who had his shit together. Instead, I was in bed with a mama's boy. I should have told him right then and there, "You need to grow up first before I can date you." I should have run for the hills. Instead, I went to dinner.

It wasn't long after this that he broke up with me. I was crushed and heartbroken, but just two weeks later, I received a MySpace letter from The Guido asking for a second chance. He was all, "I miss you! You're the best thing I ever had." Again, only a stupid-ass doormat would jump on this. That would be me. I went back with him and it was the biggest mistake of my life. I spent six more months with this loser; I even moved into his small-ass apartment. That's when I got an up-close and personal view of what an asshole looks like in action.

First, I learned that that his mom paid for his car as well as most of his bills because he was "between jobs." It's tough, after all, to hold down a paying job when you're out all night clubbing. Then, the day I was moving stuff into his place, my dog Bella grabbed The Guido's wallet and started chewing on it. I wrestled it back from her and found a hotel receipt inside. It was dated the month before, exactly the time The Guido told me he was visiting his poor dying grandmother in Italy. Only this receipt wasn't from Italy; it said "Acapulco" on it, along with a girl's e-mail address and number on the back.

I thought fast; I needed more evidence. So I searched MySpace with the girl's e-mail address and BAM! There she was in pictures with her hands all over my boy-friend! I wanted to scream. My adrenaline was pumping out of control, and I was actually afraid I was going to run upstairs and punch him in the face. But first I needed to call this girl and get the scoop.

I started to tell her who I was, but she beat me to it: "How's your dog Bella doing?" she asked. "I know all about you, and just to let you know, while your boy was supposed to be in Italy, he was really down in Mexico fucking me." Bitch. When I hung up the phone, I was shaking and I ran to throw up. It took me a few minutes to regain my composure before I went upstairs and confronted him. Now, I know this doesn't sound like the JWOWW you see on *Jersey Shore*: a tough-as-nails, take-no-prisoners bitch who would never let a man walk all over her like this. But I wasn't the same person when I knew The Guido. I wasn't strong, and I kept letting things escalate.

As I told him the conversation I had just had, The Guido stared at me with this blank look on his face. Then he laughed. I started to cry—another big mistake, because it shows a guy how vulnerable you are. I was sobbing when he said, "So, you want these movers to turn around?" I couldn't grasp it. I had to leave. I ran out to my car and it wouldn't start. Shit! I had to get outta there. So I called my best friend to have her jump it, and I just sat in my car waiting for her, crying over my steering wheel.

It was a big pity party. I wondered what I had done to bring this on myself. Did he cheat because I wasn't good enough for him? I hit such a low point. I went back to my friend's that night but came crawling back to him the next day. I put my shit in his house. I knew things would never be the same—there is no real way of repairing a relationship after someone cheats. But I just couldn't let ago. I allowed the future disgusting events to happen to me.

Once I moved in, I noticed a bunch of things: first off, he hid his cell phone while he slept—so I couldn't see what other whores he was calling and texting. He also had lots of different MySpace accounts, filled with pictures of him hooking up with different girls. And every time I left town to see my family, I'd come home to a clean bedroom. Why? He washed the bedding since he was fucking another girl in it while I was away. It took until Fourth of July weekend to build the strength I needed to walk away from him. And that was when I hit rock bottom. He told me he was leaving for a couple of hours with his friends and it turned into three days. He wouldn't even answer my calls. I cried that entire weekend in our apartment. Why was he so cruel to me? I did everything I could for this guy and forgave him for everything so he could treat me like shit? I knew deep down I was such an amazing girlfriend to him, and yet he kept walking all over me and disrespecting me.

That's when it clicked . . . I needed to get the fuck out of there. I packed my shit, took my dog, and left him. My friends and I were busy moving my stuff out when The Guido strolled in on July 7, looking guilty. All my girls scrammed like cockroaches; I think they had a hunch it was about to get ugly.

"It's over, right?" he said. I got so mad. I mean *really*? How fucking heartless are you? I love you and this is what I get? I started screaming and crying. "I called every hospital and precinct making sure you weren't hurt or arrested," I told him. No such luck; he was fucking some whore out east. Then things got ugly. Looking back, I don't think it should have gone down like that. But everything happens for a reason, and so be it.

After it was over, I couldn't cry. I couldn't cry because I knew I did it to myself. I allowed this guy to walk all over me. I had all the warning signs and I ignored them. But like I said, it taught me a lesson. I was finally free from The Guido—and a little smarter from having been to battle.

Since then, I've learned a shit load about dating. On *Jersey Shore*, I learned even more, from long-distance relationships with guys to creeping at the club. I wish someone had given me a book—or a crash course—that showed me what to watch out for. They should probably teach a class in high school or college, "Fucked-up Typical Jerk-offs 101," so we can all steer clear.

SIX SIGNS HE'S A CHEATING SCUMBAG

....

If any of these are creeping into your relationship, be suspicious. If all six are happening—honey, kick his ass to the curb!

Physical evidence. Phone numbers crammed in his pockets; lipstick on his T-shirt collar; some cheap clip-on hair in his bed.

Verbal evidence. He gets defensive when you ask him where he's been; he has a million excuses for why he didn't call when he said he would; his stories reek of bullshit—he tells you he was at the gym but he didn't have his sneakers with him and he's fresh to death. Hmmmm.

The sex has slowed down. If he ain't pounding you more than once a month, what is his dick doing the other twenty-nine days?

He keeps talking about someone else. Maybe a female coworker, his buddy Joey's little sister, the cleaning lady. This bitch just keeps coming up in conversation. Why is he so interested? Well, what the fuck do you think?

He takes a lot of trips. For business, with his friends, fishing with his uncle Luigi. His bag always seems to be packed. Check it for Trojans.

You feel it in your gut. You can't explain it, but you just sense something is up (probably his dick!) and you feel your relationship falling apart at the scams. I'm not saying be paranoid. But if you suddenly seem to lose the connection between you—he doesn't laugh or smile with you, or hold your hand—then there's a damn good reason. Usually it has tits.

RULE 15: DON'T FUCK UP THE FIRST DATE

Not too long ago, pre-Perfection, I was having dinner with this good-looking guy that I had been dying to go out with. We sat down and I was thinking, "Nice! This guy is hot!" I was totally into him, then he dropped a bomb right at the table: he told me he was twenty-eight and still lived at home with his mommy. And worse: he *liked* living at home with her and having her take care of him, cook his meals, do his laundry, etc. He wasn't at all embarrassed by that fact or trying to get his own place. Cricket central. I couldn't think of a thing to say to him after that because I was so turned off. I just kept picturing us having sex while his mother watched. I lost my appetite.

He made one of the most common and deadly mistakes men and women make on the first date: he aired his dirty-ass laundry. Too much information, too soon. I'm not saying lie, but at least have enough common sense to self-edit. For fucking crying out loud, give your date some time to get to know you before you let slip that your mom is still wiping your ass!

It's easy to screw up a first date—no one is perfect, including yours truly. So how do you make the first date go smooth and keep him/her wanting more?

DON'T DIG TOO MUCH INTO THE PAST

It is none of your beeswax at this point how many girls he's slept with or how/why he screwed up old relationships. And he sure as hell doesn't need to know that you were once a hundred pounds heavier and went to fat camp (he'll just try to picture it . . . not a turn-on!) or that you have an irrational fear of frogs (say what you want . . . they freak me out!). Look, everyone has their own shit to deal with. These are things that you gradually open up about as your relationship deepens. Not stuff you blurt out when you're just getting to know someone.

BE CAREFUL HOW MUCH YOU DRINK

Do I need to remind you how Snooks made a horrible first impression on all of us at the *Shore* house because she got wasted? Too much booze loosens lips—and not in a good way. I know that first dates are nerve-racking and drinking calms you down, but pace yourself. Don't keep knocking 'em back or your date is going to think you're sloppy. You want him to call you again—not call AA for you.

MAKE EASY CONVERSATION

I like to make sure that for every question I answer, I ask one back. That's a good balance. Try to avoid those awkward long pauses of silence where you can hear your stomach growling. Keep it light and simple: you can talk about your work, your hobbies (unless they're kinky or illegal), music, sports, the freakin' weather if you have to. If you've just graduated college, then you can say where, when, and what you studied—don't dwell on all the wild drunken frat parties you went to or mention that you gave your philosophy professor a lap dance so you could pass his class. Do not—I repeat, do not get into politics or religion; you're not looking to start a huge argument the first date, and these topics often ignite strong opinions. This can turn a great first night to crap really fast.

PAY ATTENTION

Maintain eye contact and don't zone out. Even if you're bored shitless, act like you care about his comic-book collection. Smile, nod your head in approval, throw in an occasional "really?," "no shit!," or "uh-huh . . ." so he knows you're following. Resist the urge to text or check voice mail/e-mail or your makeup. Major no-no. It sends off signals that you are uninterested. I would never talk to a guy again if he was on his phone bullshitting to someone while he's on a date with me. My time is valuable, and that's how you should make the other person feel, too.

BE CONFIDENT

Even if you're not as big a loudmouth as I am, you can still keep your head up, back straight, and smile. Don't slouch, look at your feet, or twirl your hair nervously. Guys pick up on that. There may be hotter girls than you at this restaurant/club, but you need to act like you're the hottest, hands down. Make him realize he has a confident chick by his side, or you know what? He *will* stare at your competition and lose sight of what's in front of him.

DON'T TALK ABOUT YOURSELF
THE WHOLE TIME

He'll think you're a conceited bitch. Even if, like me, you're proud of all your hard work and how much you've accomplished, tone it down a notch. Don't act like you're Miss Independent and don't need a man in your life—because he'll get that message loud and clear and take off. Let him get a word in every now and then; don't monopolize the conversation. Show him you need and want his opinion. Men like to feel important; they have fragile little egos that need to be stroked. Suck it up and act like you think he's God's gift. It will go a long way.

DON'T DO ANYTHING YOU SUCK AT

Plain and simple: if you are a sloppy, blackout drunk, avoid meeting up for drinks on your first date. Suggest a coffeehouse instead or someplace where alcohol is not being waved in your face. You do not want to show that side of you. If you are a horrible singer, don't go to a karaoke bar and give the guy a headache with your sorry-ass Lady Gaga imitation. Stick to what you're good at doing. Again, it's all about airing your dirty laundry. Save the fact that you're tone-deaf till you solidify the relationship (and can buy him earplugs).

RULE 16: SPELL OUT WHAT YOU WANT

When you enter into a relationship, I believe you should make it clear from the start what you expect. You can either let this unfold a little bit more with each date, or wait till you've been out on a few of them before speaking up. Basically, the time to do it is before you're in too deep. You don't want to be on the road and have to slam on the brakes. I'm always honest with the guy. I don't go as far as Snook does, writing up her list of must-haves ("a tan juicehead gorilla nympho who isn't a jerk-off; smells good; likes pickles, romantical, likes to sleep in . . ."). But I do make it apparent during the first handful of dates what I need to get out of this. And that's respect: no lies, no cheating, no treating me like a piece of shit when your buddies are around.

I am also not in the market for a hookup, and you'll notice on the show I never come home with anyone. I want more than that. And maybe the guy doesn't. Maybe he doesn't want to be tied down. That's okay; better I know now than later. As long as he's open to a relationship, then I'm game to give a try. But if he's out-and-out telling me that all he's interested in is banging me . . . so long. Why am I so specific? Because I don't want to fall for a guy that I know won't work. I also don't want to get in bed with someone who's going to turn out to be pointless. So I set my standards in the beginning, and see if the guy fits the bill. If not, I tell him sorry it didn't work out and I'm not inter-ested. There's nothing wrong with being assertive—especially if you really know what you want and don't want to waste time getting it. A lot of women might be concerned that this will scare a guy off. Maybe. But if it does, he was not considering you girlfriend material to

begin with. A guy who's into you won't scare that easily. You can keep it simple: "I just wanna know if you're
looking for a girlfriend . . . or a girl to fuck." Or you
can go easier on him: "I'm not really interested in just
hooking up. I really like you. How do you feel about
that?" Either one will get you an answer.

There is only one topic I do not want you to bring
up—not on the first date, not on the second, not even
after a month of smushing a guy. That is BABIES. If you
want a child, don't mention it until you are in a relationship for months and months. No guy is sitting around
picturing himself changing diapers and burping some
screaming kid at 2 A.M. He'll get freaked out and take
off for the hills. If you can, wait till he brings it up. I
am dating someone now who is thirty-five years old and
he never in a million years thought about marriage and
kids. Then one day, he saw me with a friend's baby. He
said, "I never knew I would ever find someone I'd want
to marry and have a family with until now. And some-
day I would love that with you." It was the best feeling
in the world to hear that. But had I brought it up before,
when he wasn't even in the mind-set . . . it could have
been awkward and uncomfortable. It might have even
put a wall between us. There is a right time and a right
place to bring up bambinos. Even if it's on your mind
24/7 and that biological clock is pounding in your ears,
stifle yourself until you're sure it's something he wants
to discuss.

RULE 17: BUST HIS BALLS A LITTLE

I'm not saying torture the poor sap for fun—just make him work for it. You can go about this in several ways. First off, be a woman of mystery. This drives men ape-shit. Never tell your whole life story in one night. Reveal it slowly, like peeling away the layers of an onion. Just say enough to make him interested. As a rule, you also always want to play up the positive. Steer clear of conversations about your psycho boss, your bitchy roommate, or your previous boyfriends, particularly their prowess in the bedroom. You may think that talking about other guys will make your man jealous and push him to be with you more, but it's actually a huge turn-off. No guy wants to be banging you and worrying that you're comparing the size of his dick to your ex's.

Another great tactic is to keep him waiting. Always be a few minutes late—it's a woman's prerogative. When Ramona the pole dancer from Tantra stood up Vin, it made him crazy—but he went crawling back, begging for more. She was even forty-five minutes late for their last night in Miami—the woman's got skills. If you show up ahead of time, it signals desperation and willingness to bow down to the guy. It's also a good idea not to be too "available" when he wants you. Let him think he has to take a number. When he calls, it's okay not to pick up on the first ring and let him leave a message. If you're too quick, he'll think you're staring at your phone, waiting for him to hit you up. Same goes for texts—you shouldn't always be the first one to send one. It's the sign of a clinger. And don't always let him call the shots and make the plans. If he is available Tuesday, you are available Thursday. Even if you have nothing going on that night, offer another night just to see how badly he wants to see you.

I only caution you that when following this rule, don't overdo it. The idea is to be a seductive puzzle he wants to figure out—not a pain in the ass. You don't want him to think you're blowing him off or yanking his chain too hard. Leave him hanging a little bit, just not enough to fall off.

RULE 18: MAKE HIM PAY

If he is interested, he is interested enough to ensure you eat well and get home safely in a cab. No cheap bastard makes a good boyfriend. Even though it's 2011, that doesn't mean a guy can't pay for dinner. I get that women want to establish equality in a relationship—but I don't think we should get stuck with the fucking tab all the time. Besides, guys like to pay. It makes them feel powerful and in control. Take that away from him, and you're cutting off his dick.

If he doesn't know what a florist is, dump him. That might be harsh, but you know what I'm saying here. He needs to at least show up every now and then with a small token. It doesn't have to be flowers, but some sort of gift. Drop a hint and see if he gets it; it shows that he is paying attention to you and cares. So if you say, "I love teddy bears," you better receive a freakin' teddy sooner rather than later. If he completely ignores what you say, then obviously he doesn't give a shit (or needs his hearing checked?) and you need to find someone that does.

GOODIES GIRLS LOVE

....

In case your man needs a less than subtle hint, you might want to highlight this section and show it to him.

- **Flowers.** Roses—the long-stemmed kind; not carnations or daisies or something you just ripped out of your neighbor's backyard. Remember how Vinny and Pauly went to a nice florist and asked for pricey bouquets for their chicks? Smooth move!

- **Lingerie.** Sexy, skimpy, lacy, leaving little to the imagination. If you show up with granny panties, it better be a joke . . .

- **Tickets to a cool concert, a sporting event, a show.** Even better if you've done your research and figured out when my fave band/team is playing local.

- **Jewelry.** Frankly, a guy can never go wrong with something that sparkles. Some nice hoops, a cool watch . . .

- **Clothing or accessories** from my favorite store. Serious points for this one, because it shows you've been paying attention to my style!

- **Anything with a label.** A bag, a pair of boots, a belt. Something statusy that I can show off to my girls and brag about how generous you are.

- **A card for no occasion**—especially one that says I love you. Perfection gives me one when I least expect it, and it makes me melt. He tucks it in my luggage or leaves it next to me on the pillow.

RULE 19: DON'T SMUSH TOO SOON

Sex early in your dating game plan will ruin everything. I take this one seriously. I will not sleep with someone unless I know they're fully into me—I don't care how much he begs. There's no set time for how long you should wait; some girls feel the four-date rule works well, while others get down to The Business at the one-month mark. My advice is to hold out for as long as you can—you need to both feel comfortable and confident that you're ready to take things to the next level. If he thinks you're too easy, he'll get turned off. A girl who puts out without much of a protest is just no fun. Men like the tug-of-war; they like to feel like getting into your pants is a challenge, a game they need to win. I went out with Perfection for weeks before I gave it up at the *Shore* house. So draw it out; sweat him. A couple of cold showers won't kill a guy. Also be aware that sex changes things. You've been intimate, and that brings with it certain expectations in the relationship. It colors the way you see each other—even with your clothes on. Once you've done the dirty, there's no going back. For more sex tips, see Chapter 9.

RULE 20: DIRTY TALK IS FINE; A DIRTY GUY ISN'T

MVP set the rule on this one—you will never see my roommates going out without sprucing up and pulling on a nice T-shirt. My man better look mint or I am looking elsewhere. Things like hygiene and clothing—the way a man treats himself—are a telltale sign of how he will treat you. If he can't comb his hair or brush his teeth after he scarfs down a slice of pepperoni, you think you're going to get any TLC in a relationship? Okay, sometimes a guy is clueless. You can take him shopping at Ed Hardy. But a skank is a skank; there's not much you can do about that. My girlfriend once dated a guy who didn't understand what a Laundromat was or what it was used for. As a result, he reeked. I mean like the rotted cheese sandwich under the car mat that made Ronnie wanna hurl. If you really like the guy (and I don't know why you would in this case . . .), tell him to clean up his act. If he doesn't, then he needs to get his smelly ass out of your time zone.

RULE 21: MAKE IT CLEAR THAT YOU ARE NUMERO UNO

If I'm on a date, I do not want to see my guy give some blond bitch at the bar fuck-me eyes. And if we're progressing into the next stage—a relationship—then I should be the center of his universe, plain and simple. Do not let me catch you scoping someone out, or worse, talking to some slut while I'm taking a leak in the ladies'. Not only is this rude in my book, but if it happens repeatedly, it's grounds for dismissal. I know men like to look and some women are okay with this—no harm, no foul. But at this stage in the game, if they're looking they're also probably touching, too. Then you're in a Ronnie-Sammi situation. And, girlfriend, I do not want to have to spell it out to you in a letter!

I get that guys—even married ones—can't help

noticing a hot girl walk in the room. I like to turn heads myself! And I understand that a man's penis often overrides all common sense. But a quick, appreciative glance is one thing; his tongue wiping up the floor, or even worse, a verbal acknowledgment ("Damn, she is hot!") is another story. Dude, keep it to yourself. You can think it, but I don't want to hear it or see it—it makes me feel like the leftover food in the back of the fridge I had to clean out in Miami. As far as I'm concerned, I am all you need and more, so there is no need to be looking elsewhere.

The way I see it, if you notice your date ogling another woman, you have two possible ways to handle it:

1. **Laugh and make a joke.** You can say, "Excuse me? Would you like a Bounty to wipe up that drool?" He'll likely get embarrassed and stop.

2. **Give him a warning.** Politely (that means without nagging, bitching, or ripping him a new asshole) tell him you noticed his gaze wandering and it's not cool with you. Eyes on the prize—not the whores. 'Nuf said.

Dear JWOWW:

My boyfriend is always comparing me to other women. He'll say stuff like, "Why don't you wear a nice sexy top like that?" or "Why don't you wear your hair in a pouf like her?" What should I do?

Let's see, you have two options: 1. Punch him in the mouth; 2. Tell him to stick a sock in it. The latter is more polite but probably not as effective but I wouldn't recommend the first. Seriously, why is he making you feel inferior? If he's your boyfriend, not only should he be building you up, he should truly believe you are the hottest thing since Tabasco sauce. I would question his motivation. Is he trying to tell you he's not happy with you on his arm, or is he simply offering to pay for an upgrade— i.e., buy you a smokin' new wardrobe and some hair extensions? Call him on it. And if that fails, then point out some Guido with a six-pack on the dance floor and say, "Why can't you have a body like that?" If he can't take it, he shouldn't dish it out.

CHAPTER 4

RELATIONSHIPS

RULE 22: IN A GUY'S MIND,
MONOGAMY EQUALS MONOTONY

A lot of relationship problems start when you get a little too comfortable. All of a sudden it's "same shit, different day." Guys hate feeling trapped in a routine, and for many, that's why they cheat. Sometimes they're not even discriminating about whom they cheat with—it's just a different hole to put his dick into, and that alone is worth the price of admission. My advice to you is to constantly switch things up. Keep him guessing; make the relationship full of surprises. There needs to be a different flavor than vanilla on the menu. Show up one night and do a sexy striptease; surprise him with a vacation or a day out doing something you've never done before. Order in Mexican if you usually call for pizza. Anything that is out of the ordinary—no matter how small—prevents boredom from setting in. Men are like little kids; they need to constantly be entertained with new toys.

My boyfriend will probably kill me—and Macy's might never let me in their stores again—but I gotta share one creative example of the element of surprise. One day, me and my boyfriend were looking for a suit for him. He asked me to come into the dressing and help him fit it, give my opinion, etc. He took his shirt off, then his pants off . . . and before you know it, I was taking my pants off! You get where I'm going with this! It was not expected and he was amazed; he was talking about it for weeks on end. So the moral of this Macy's sex romp? Go where the moment takes you. That excitement of the unexpected is going to make your relationship last forever.

RULE 23: DON'T KNOCK YOURSELF OFF THE PEDESTAL

You may well have all the bodily functions of a man, but you should not demonstrate them in the early stages of a relationship. Guys gross out easily. Burping, farting, and all that stuff is disgusting. They can do it; they take fucking pride in it. But a girl is not supposed to be nasty. The image of you doing something foul becomes seared into a guy's brain. Guys prefer to think that women are perfect—we don't take dumps or shave our armpits or pick our noses. And if that's what they choose to believe,

I say support them in it. Until you get to know each other much, much better, make him think you are a goddess who never passes gas.

RULE 24: KISS HIS MOTHER'S ASS

Never, ever criticize his mother unless you want to remain single. Most men—particularly Italian ones—are tight with their mamas (Vinny calls his a saint). You need to get on her good side at every opportunity and never challenge her opinion or her authority. At the end of the day, no matter how much he loves you, his mama can make or break your relationship with him. If she likes you, she'll push him to settle down and propose. And if it gets ugly between you and her, let's be real: who do you think he will choose, the woman who gave him life or some girl he's screwing? Always be polite, always bring gifts, always tell her she looks fabulous. If you have to suck up to his mother to seal the deal . . . so be it. If she's a total bitch, wait till after the wedding to put her in her place.

RULE 25: IF IT SMELLS LIKE A HOOKUP . . .
IT IS A HOOKUP

I have seen a lot of my friends fall into this trap and I was guilty of it with The Guido: you think you're in a relationship with some guy—you even believe he's your boyfriend—but to him, you're just a hookup. What does this mean? Basically, if he's got an itch, he knows he can call and you'll come running to scratch it. Ladies, if you actually allow yourself to be this girl, you need to get slapped upside the head with some confidence! No woman should see these signs and stick around if she has a shred of self-respect. I know sometimes it's tough— you really are hot for this jerk and try to overlook the "issues" in your relationship because the sex is mind-blowing. I get it. Been there, done that. But after a while, you have to ask yourself: "Is it worth it? Is it worth being unhappy?" What is the point in continuing something that's nothing?

Maybe you believe you can change him. A leopard doesn't change his spots and a hookup artist doesn't get down on one knee. But if you want to prove me wrong, then try this little experiment: the next time he places a booty call to you, tell him you have another date you're really excited about and see how he reacts. Make up some crazy-ass story: "Yeah, Sergio is picking me up in his BMW after he's done with his surgeries for the day . . ." When threatened with real competition—namely, a man who's smarter, richer, and cooler than him—he might just step up his game and be the man you want. If not, he's a prick and move on.

SIX SIGNS YOU'RE A HOOKUP

Sign 1: He never takes you out in public

Basically, he doesn't want to be seen with your ass. If he only hangs out with you at his place and barely comes to you (your house), then walk away. He obviously has issues with the relationship if he's hiding you in the closet from his roommates. I'm sorry, but any man I'm dating better be damn proud to show me off. He should take out a billboard in Times Square as far as I'm concerned.

Sign 2: He never spends any money on you

He doesn't take you to dinner or buy you anything. This is basically solidifying "I'm only using you for sex and you will never get anything from me." Like Ronnie says, "You get dick and bubble gum . . . that's all." I'm not saying he needs to be showering you with jewels and designer bags. But hey, it doesn't hurt! A relationship is an investment; he needs to invest the time and sometimes the cash as well.

Sign 3: He never introduces you to his friends or family

He probably won't even mention them or tell you their names. I had a friend who was dating some guy for six months before she accidentally bumped into one of his sisters (she saw her name on a credit card and asked if they were related) at a tanning salon. The sister said, "Didn't you know he has six sisters?" My girlfriend was stunned; she didn't have a clue because he'd never mentioned it. That is just wrong—and a telltale sign in my book. He doesn't want you to know shit about his life and/or what he does. That doesn't sound too suspicious, now, does it?

Sign 4: He doesn't want you on his networking site like Facebook or MySpace

Again, this is a move to keep you out of his business and away from his friends and family (who would maybe tell you how many women he's actually sleeping with). Or even worse: he does friend you but blatantly flirts with other girls on there and completely doesn't even acknowledge your presence.

Sign 5: He only calls you/wants to see you really late

This basically states, "Listen, I couldn't find a girl to bring home tonight, so I need you to come over and be second best." Unless he's a vampire, he can see you in the daylight. You're no one's backup bitch!

Sign 6: He's always unavailable/makes excuses when you want to hang out

Isn't it amazing how no matter what you ask him to do—or how much notice you give him—he always has a prior commitment, a pressing engagement, a crisis that just came up? It's never his fault, of course. If you believe that, I have a nice bridge I'd like to sell you.

RULE 26: A GUY'S BRAINS ARE LOCATED BELOW THE BELT

Let me be perfectly clear on this: a man thinks with his penis and is always on a quest for one thing and one thing only: sex. Once you grasp this concept and make peace with it, you will understand what makes him do the things he does. Like make out with a strange woman at a bar while he's been on the dance floor with you all night. Or climb in the hot tub with some skank he hardly knows. You are not dealing with a rational-behaving individual. You're dealing with a dick. This is why you always have to be on top of your game physically and emotionally. He likes you because of how confident you are and how your sex appeal turns him on. So never lose those aspects of yourself.

So if this is the case, then what would make a man choose quality over quantity? If he can have a hundred girls in his bed, why settle for just one? According to my *Shore* mates, occasionally, a specific girl, "a rare rose," as Vinny and Pauly call it, crosses his path and makes him go all romantic. As Vin so eloquently put it, "If you got a good woman at home, you just say no to the ho." And what does this good woman possess (besides serious skills):

SHE'S A NICE GIRL

Someone like me (LOL) or maybe someone that reminds him of his mother. When guys are ready to settle down, they can be very picky about it. Especially if these guys (like my roommates) are successful and good-looking and have girls throwing themselves at them day and night. So a girl has to really demonstrate that she's high caliber all the way—a class act. Vinny says it's the kind of girl he can imagine introducing to his family. Basically, there are girls you bed and girls you wed. Guys want a girl who demonstrates morals—in a nutshell, no one who picks out pj's from Mike's closet on the first date.

SHE NURTURES HIM

Men are all big babies; they want a woman to care for them and coddle them, to defend them and devote themselves to them—again, it's all about Mama. I am a ride-or-die bitch, and I am still willing to take care of my man. I don't consider it a chore; I like to make him feel special. That is no way a sign of weakness. A lot of women are not like that anymore. They think it's the twenty-first century, so they don't have to play the nuturer. Well, that's why they're still single. A guy goes ape-shit over a woman who cares for him—remember the Canadian chick in the club who told another bitch to keep her hands off Mike? He was speechless. He loved that she was "protecting" him. I'm not saying you have to wipe his ass or wash his sweaty T-shirts, but a few gestures that show you care will go a long way. There should always be a balance of independence and having people depend on you.

SHE HAS A LIFE

No guy wants to feel like he's being choked to death in a relationship. Stage 5 clingers and stalkers are an instant turn-off. A woman who has things to do, places to go, people to see . . . she's got wife potential. This isn't to say she blows her guy off—let's get the priorities straight. In my roommates' minds, when they call, a girl should come running. But when they're out doing GTL, this woman's not whining or complaining or demanding more face time. She's got her own individual existence beyond being someone's girlfriend.

RULE 27: IF HE'S TREATING YOU LIKE PINOCCHIO, CUT THE STRINGS

Translation: you should never allow yourself to be anyone's puppet. I had to learn this the hard way (what else is new?). I was dating this guy for a year, let's call him "The Mistake"—when suddenly he started getting very insecure in our relationship. He wanted me to spend more time with him and him only, and that meant cutting all my guy and girl friends out of the picture. That's right, he wanted to dictate who I saw, what I did, where I went. Total fucking control freak. He stayed in Jersey five days a week for work, but before I knew it, he had moved into my house in Long Island so he could totally be up my ass. He kept saying it was because I needed him to be around; I was lonely. I wasn't fucking lonely; I was sick of him. He didn't want me to go out or have fun without him there to supervise. I couldn't take a shit without him wanting to watch (or at least it felt that way). I felt like I was falling down this black hole, losing myself little by little, till there was nothing left. I mentally shut down. I was exhausted. I felt like I was in *Invasion of the Body Snatchers*. But I couldn't get away that easy because I made the second biggest mistake: I allowed him to work with me. What the fuck was wrong with me? Did I not see this guy was bad news from the start? Did I not realize he was possessing me and destroying everything about my life that I loved? When I was around him, I wasn't myself. I felt like a shadow of the person I used to be, a numb, depressed, empty shell. And that is no way to exist nor is it a healthy relationship.

After I'd dated a guy who sucked the joy out of my life like a Hoover vacuum, there is no way I would ever make this "Mistake" again. I know now that a relationship is made up of two people—not one who is calling all the shots and pulling your strings like some freakin' puppet. Sometimes when you think you're in love, you don't notice yourself slipping away. Then one day you walk by a mirror and think, "Who the fuck is that? That can't be me!" But it is. And that's when it's time to pick up whatever shred of self-respect you have left and haul your ass out of there. Thankfully, that's what I finally did. My friends wanted to throw a party, they were so happy that it was over.

What you need to know is why a guy tries to control you. In a word: fear. He is terrified that you are in some way, or even many ways, better, smarter, hotter than him. He's afraid you're going to cheat on him or leave him because he doesn't measure up. This type of guy isn't always a bad person; he may simply not like himself. Too bad you get stuck making up for it. Looking back now, I can see the signs were all there . . .

FIVE RED FLAGS THAT HE'S A CONTROL FREAK

1. **He's clingy**. He wants to be with you 24/7. If you disappear for too long, he texts/calls you to see where you are and who you're with.

2. **He doesn't trust you**. He secretly checks your cell phone, e-mails, goes through your purse and address book, pumps your friends for info, and spies on you when you go out.

3. **He wants you all to himself**. This means isolating you from your friends, family, work mates. He doesn't want anyone around you that might convince you he's bad news.

4. **He lays on a guilt trip**. Whenever you try to do anything he's not involved in or something he doesn't approve of (namely, have a life!), he spreads it on thick. Even worse, he adds on moping, sighing, puppy-dog eyes—or storms out of the room like you've done him wrong. The goal is to make you feel like crap so you don't do it again.

5. **He knocks you down**. He tries to make you feel like a loser so you become more dependent on him. He's constantly criticizing, chipping away at your confidence. When you put on a few pounds (because he's driving you to eat for consolation), his pet name for you is "Willy." As in the whale.

RULE 28: IF THERE'S TROUBLE, TALK ABOUT IT

Every *Cosmo* article will tell you how important it is to communicate. This isn't bullshit; you cannot expect to be in a relationship and not talk. Shit happens; stuff goes wrong. One of you might wind up feeling hurt, deceived, dicked around. If there's a problem, you guys need to talk about it. If not, it will just grow there like a tumor.

It may not be an easy conversation—you think Ronnie wanted to tell Sam he was at a bar with two other girls—but it needs to happen. My feeling is this: I am going to be pissed at you if you did something wrong, but I will be even more pissed at you (and probably never forgive you) if I have to hear it from somebody else. Because that is humiliating. That basically tells me you don't care enough about me to be honest.

The Mistake had a lovely habit of walking away when things got tense between us. Why talk about it? That might mean acknowledging that he did something wrong. The sound of silence between us was sometimes deafening. That's not fighting fair. If you get things out in the open, at least you know where you stand. I know conflict isn't fun, but it's better than keeping feelings bottled up inside till you both explode.

FIVE WAYS TO FIGHT RIGHT

....

1. **Make an appointment.** If one or both of you are avoiding the subject, you need to schedule a sit-down. Arrange a place and time and put it on the book. Say, "Listen, we need to talk. When is good for you?" Make sure you don't have an audience (a restaurant is probably not the best idea—nor is the living room in your Shore house). This should be

a private, one-on-one session, with no time limit. If you're both busy, then find a time on a weekend when things are slower and you're not rushing to work.

2. **Have the right attitude.** You want to come at this in a positive way. You're not blaming or accusing, you're going to work this out together as a couple because you care about each other. Coming at it from this direction will make him less intimidated and the conversation will be easier.

3. **Listen up.** Don't just wail on his ass without giving him the opportunity to explain and say how he feels—tempting as that may be. Even if you're not liking what he's telling you, he deserves to have the floor for a few minutes. If you don't hear him out, the next time something comes between you, he'll just figure he's better off keeping his mouth shut.

4. **Don't get defensive.** If you're on the receiving end—and you didn't do anything wrong—it's hard not to get pissed off and protest. But if all you do is deny, deny, deny, you're basically telling him you don't give a shit how he feels. You may not have done the act, but something (or someone) has caused him to think you did. There is some serious

miscommunication going on between you. You
need to acknowledge his feelings and keep your
cool. You can say something like "I hear you" or "I
realize you're upset" to steer the conversation away
from "You did . . . no, I didn't!" Once he sees that
you care, explain what really happened.

5. **Play nice**. By this, I mean no low blows in the
conversation. Don't bring up his past mistakes or
problems, don't threaten to call his mother, don't
call him names. Act like an adult, for fucking
crying out loud! It's like when Snook asked for a
roll at dinner in AC and Mike snapped back, "You
already got a couple." Uncalled for. It hurt her
feelings and made the tension between them even
worse. Keep the smart-ass remarks under your hat;
they're not funny, and they're not going to help you
work things out between you. And it goes without
saying that you should NEVER get physical. No
punching him in the face, no throwing a plate
at his shit-talking mug, no kicking him where it
hurts. If you have to, take a walk around the block
to cool down. If you're too pissed, you're better off
tabling the talk until the steam stops pouring out of
your ears. Broken bones are not going to heal your
relationship. Just sayin' . . .

RULE 29: WHEN YOU'RE SURE HE'S THE ONE, SLAP ON THE CUFFS

Commitment scares the shit out of guys. To them, it's not about finding a lifelong partner to love you. It's about giving up everything that makes them a man: the partying, the hooking up, the freedom to do whatever they damn please whenever they want with whomever they want. Which presents a huge problem: you're ready to be in a long-term—maybe even till-death-do-us-part—relationship, and he feels like you're putting the nail in his coffin. Ladies, there is a formula to be followed. There is a four-step program (tested and approved by me) that will not only have him melting like butter in your hands but will make him want to stop looking. Now, this might stir up some controversy; independent, modern women will accuse me of being too old school in my approach. But I'm a successful, modern woman who kicks ass and I don't have a problem with it.

This isn't being submissive; it's actually a power play where you're learning to manipulate a guy's thoughts and emotions. If you understand how guys tick, you know how to set the clock. It's just my opinion and you're entitled to yours. Say what you want, but I'm not shitting you; it works!

Cook for him . . .

and cook really well. If you don't know how to cook, you better learn because a man wants a wife that makes a feast—not reservations. It's like that old saying "The way to a man's heart is through his stomach." Believe it. Sex and food are all a guy needs to make him happy. When you cook for him, do it in front of him. Let him watch you slicing and dicing and let him taste. Make his mouth water. For the menu, I recommend a good Italian dinner from scratch. Sausage and peppers. Grilled vegetables. Chicken cutlets. Penne à la vodka. Make sure there's wine or champagne to go with the food. Show that there's more to you than partying and going to clubs—you can be all domestic. If you cook for him at his house, clean up everything after dinner.

The first time I spent the night at my man's house, we made a mess everywhere. So when he went to work the next morning, I slept in and went to town on his place. It fucking sparkled. So after a long day at work, he came home to a spotless house and dinner on the table. He was speechless. He couldn't believe that I cared that much about him. Guys really appreciate things like that; they think this type of woman doesn't exist anymore. Prove them wrong.

THE FIRST MEAL I COOKED FOR MR. PERFECTION

· ·

A homemade Italian meal . . . for a guy, it can be just as good as sex. Serve up with a nice loaf of Italian bread, cut thin and buttered. You can be dessert.

PENNE À LA VODKA

7 cloves garlic, minced
1 onion, diced
3 whole tomatoes, chopped
3 tablespoons olive oil
1 (28-ounce) can whole peeled
   tomatoes
12-ounce can tomato paste
1 cup chopped fresh basil
Salt and pepper to taste
½ cup vodka
1 pint heavy cream
1 pound penne pasta

1. In a large skillet over medium heat, cook the garlic, onion, and tomatoes (fresh) in olive oil until tender (about 1 to 2 minutes). Stir in the canned tomatoes and tomato paste, breaking up a bit with a fork. Stir in the basil, salt, and pepper and simmer for 15 minutes. Stir in the vodka and allow the flame to burn out. Cook for 15 minutes more.

2. Take ¼ of the sauce and set aside for the top of the chicken Parm (see opposite).

3. Stir in cream to the remainder of the sauce and simmer for 10 minutes. Turn off the heat.

4. Bring a large pot of water to a boil. Add to it a pinch of salt and $\frac{1}{3}$ teaspoon of olive oil. Add the pasta and cook for 8 to 10 minutes or until al dente; drain.

5. Toss the hot pasta in the sauce.

CHICKEN PARM

2 eggs, beaten
1 cup flour
4 ounces dry bread crumbs
4 skinless, boneless chicken
    breast halves

1 cup olive oil
Leftover sauce from penne à la
    vodka recipe
4 ounces shredded mozzarella
$\frac{1}{4}$ cup grated Parmesan cheese

1. Preheat oven to 350° F. Lightly grease a medium-size baking sheet.

2. Pour the eggs into a small shallow bowl. Spread the flour over a large plate. Place the bread crumbs in a separate shallow bowl. Assembly-line style, dredge the chicken in the egg until it is fully covered (let the egg drip off), then dredge in the flour (fully covered), and then cover with bread crumbs.

3. Heat a skillet over medium heat and pour in olive oil.

4. Place the chicken in the skillet and let sizzle for 1 minute on each side.

5. Place the coated chicken on the baking sheet and bake in the preheated oven for 40 minutes, or until no longer pink and juices run clear.

6. Pour the sauce on top of chicken. Sprinkle mozzarella and Parmesan on top and return to oven for 10 minutes.

ASPARAGUS

Fresh bunch of asparagus
4 garlic cloves
¼ cup of onion

1 tomato
½ cup olive oil
Dash of salt and pepper

1. Cut the ends off the asparagus.

2. Dice the garlic, onion, and tomato and toss into skillet with olive oil over medium heat.

3. Cook for 5 minutes, then place the asparagus on top. Add the salt and pepper.

4. Put a cover on top of the skillet and let sit, stirring occasionally, for 20 minutes.

CAESAR SALAD

1 head romaine lettuce
1 cup lite Caesar dressing

1½ cups croutons
Grated Parmesan

1. Chop up romaine lettuce into bite-size pieces.

2. In a large bowl, mix romaine, dressing, and croutons.

3. Sprinkle Parmesan on top.

Be his friend

By this, I mean make sure you have things you do together, a few big common interests. Not everything in common, but some stuff you can share regularly. Maybe it's going to the gym to work out. Maybe it's horror movies. Or it could be just lying on the couch watching football and drinking beer. You get the picture: buddy up. The whole opposites-attract thing is bullshit; it never lasts. You need common ground to keep the relationship growing. You should be friends as well as lovers, which means spending quality time together, hanging out, sharing hobbies, listening to him vent about his asshole boss. Give him sympathy and support—think of how his closest pals would treat him. If all you do is smush, he's never going to see you in his future.

And speaking of smushing, you need to give it up . . .

a lot. Or at least enough. Guys think about sex every second of every day, so if you're not giving it to him, he's probably thinking about someone else who is. Now, this is for when you two are sexually active. In terms of the beginning of a relationship, I say wait a couple of weeks before you get to The Business (and wait even longer if you're a teenager!). It's good to make him want you bad. The anticipation is half the fun. Just know that when you do it, you better be a freak! (See Chapter 9 for more sex tips.) Don't be a stiff board and just lay there. Guys need to be entertained, and they need to know that having sex with you is enough and will be enough for years to come. Blow his mind and he won't look elsewhere.

Give him his space

If he tells you he needs a guys' night out, don't turn into a possessive, nagging bitch. Give it to him . . . with pleasure. Even if you are biting your tongue the whole time and wishing he would just stay home and snuggle you, suck it up and let him go. This is a big test for guys. They will push this situation on you to see your reaction. They want to gauge if committing to you means giving up their old life and all the things they love to do—like hang with the boys. If you're cool with it, they'll be cool with committing. They feel like you're giving them enough slack, and that marriage down the road won't be a death sentence. Smile and say, "Have a great night, baby, and text me when you can . . ." Doing that will blow his mind. And try not to worry about him cheating if he's been a good guy up to this point. I talked to a lot of guys about this subject, and they all agree that they wouldn't cheat because they feel they have a great girl at home and wouldn't want to screw it up. A girl who gives a guy freedom is gold.

Dear JWOWW:

I've been seriously dating this guy for six months now and he keeps telling me we're both free to see other people. I don't want to see other people! What should I do?

Who is he trying to convince—you or him? When a guy says shit like this, it's for one of three reasons:

1. He's freaking out that he's in deep.

2. He cheated on you and doesn't want to feel guilty about it.

3. He wants to see your reaction. Will you get jealous? Will you fuck other men if you have his permission?

If you're relatively sure he's been faithful (i.e., you're together 24/7 and he doesn't even look at other girls), then chalk it up to his insecurity getting the best of him. Men say stupid things when they like you. It's like their brains shut down to protect them from getting hurt. If you really wanna fuck with his head, you can answer, "Oh, good. I was hoping you would say that . . ."

Or you can sit down with him and say "I want to be exclusive with you." See what he says . . .

CHAPTER 5

IT'S OVER

RULE 30: BREAKING UP IS A BITCH

If you believe what you read in fairy tales, you meet your prince and live happily ever after—case closed. I am eternally optimistic—or maybe just fucking stupid—in believing that what happens in Disney movies can come true. But if you watch *Jersey Shore*, you get a different story: you're happy, you're in love . . . then one day it all turns to shit. It sucks for us, but it does make for great TV! There are usually fights, tears, flying objects, maybe some great rebound smushing. But in the end, a breakup is a breakup: it's the cutting of ties between two people who once thought they loved each other. And you know that's gonna leave a nasty scar.

No matter how you slice it; even if you're the one doing the walking, even if you hate his ass, you're still going to feel like shit. Why? Because you invested your time, effort, emotions, and one too many Saturday nights on this guy. You might have even been in love. My heart was breaking for Nicole when she called it off with—let's just call him "The Egotistical Prick." I was proud of my little Snooks; she was strong and she knew what she wanted in a relationship (namely, not him). When he called, she cut him off before he could talk any more shit. But she was hurting. She was barely talking to any of us roommates; she seemed kind of out of it and distracted. And when we went for a walk the next day, she caved. We were standing there in the middle of the street with her sobbing on my shoulder. To see her in so much pain made me cry, too. I love that girl like she is my sister and would do anything for her, but this was something I couldn't fix or make any easier.

I know exactly how she felt that day; I have been there. I have my cried my eyes out, buried my misery in food and booze, even hooked up with rebound scum to make me forget. None of the above work. What does work is time, and lots of it. Your girls can hold your hand and tell you it will be okay, you're better off without him, but only you can make that call. You have to be ready to move on.

It was probably the hardest for me to do that with The Guido. But after all the lying and cheating I knew I needed to pack my things and move out. I cried for three days, holding my dog Bella. I could barely move. I thought my world had ended, and I would never get over him. I loved him so much and could not grasp the fact he would no longer be in my life. But then one day it got easier and I thought about him a little less. And then the next day, and the next, and so on, until one day he was hardly on my mind at all.

After dating The Guido, I became a serial dater. I dated everything from rockers that played in local bands, to The Geek, The Real Estate Agent, The Doctor, and of course, multiple Guidos. Basically any guy that smiled, looked at me—heck, had a dick—I would give my number to take me out to dinner. I realized now I was just filling a void with empty dates that would go nowhere. I know it's important to get back in the saddle, but you also need to give yourself time to heal.

SIX WAYS TO SURVIVE A BREAKUP

1. **Put space between you.** Even if you stay friends, you need to break all communication and contact when you split. Idiot that I am, I wound up working with an ex in the same club. Baaaaad idea. How do you forget someone when they're crawling up your ass? If you can't change your employment—or your zip code—then at the very least minimize how much info you share with

him. He doesn't need to know the new guy you're dating (unless you want to flaunt a hottie in his face); he doesn't need to see you bawling your eyes out in the bathroom. Sit on your hands if you have to, but don't call him, text him, or e-mail him—and stay away from the places you know he hangs out. This doesn't have to be permanent; maybe one day you can actually handle being around him. But right after you call it quits, give yourself a little distance so you're not constantly reminded of the loss. Otherwise, it's like rubbing salt in the wound.

2. **Deal with the death.** Your relationship is now extinct, so expect to go through all the emotions that come with mourning it: denial, anger, and eventually acceptance. Most people get stuck in one or two of these phases longer than the others. For me, they kind of came in waves. After several of my breakups, I alternated between "I wanna fucking kill him!" and "I wanna fucking fuck him!" before settling on "I'm so fucking over him." It's okay to feel pain and longing—at least let yourself have that. Don't be afraid to let it all out and cry your brains out. It helps.

Two of my breakups nearly killed me. The pain was unbearable, and I thought I would never be able to go on. Guess what? I did. Look at me: I'm so fine, I'm even okay to write about them! So if you're reading this now, and thinking your world is ending, believe me when I say I was there and it gets better. Nothing in life is that bad that you can't overcome it. One day you will accept the breakup and be happy again.

HOW TO GET OVER A BREAKUP (IN THREE EASY STEPS)

....

You have three days—and not a minute more—to feel sorry for yourself, then you have to get off your ass and do something to forget him:

Step 1: Cocoon. When I go through a breakup, I want to be all alone for three days and just lay in bed with a bottle of whatever and a few boxes of Kleenex. During this time, get out of my face and don't attempt to try to comfort me. I need to wallow in self-pity and misery for seventy-two hours straight.

Step 2: Hit something (not your ex). Once the initial shock has worn off, it's time to channel your emotions into a more positive outlet. I took my frustrations out at the gym. Kicking, punching, and hitting things feels *good*, I promise.

Step 3: Distract yourself. I strongly suggest you get a hobby—something to take your mind off your ex and make you feel better about yourself. Bake, paint, knit, learn to do the fucking Cha-Cha-Cha (I hear The Situation may be available for ballroom dance lessons).

....

3. **Lean on your friends and family**. Like I said, I was there for Snook and she's always been there for me. And I have my best boy bud, Joey, who knew me when I was a loser from upstate and still loved me then as he does now. I will also never forget my dad coming to Long Island and sitting up all night with me, talking and sometimes just listening the day after I left The Guido. These are the people who will be your rocks and your superheroes when everything else turns to shit. It's a huge comfort to me to know this. I feel like no matter what, I have people who love me and I love them back. No jerk-off can take that away from me. When I broke up with The Mistake, Snooks was there for me. I wasn't really upset that it was over—I knew my time with

him was up—but I was distraught over his actions
during the breakup. He was heartless and wanted to
make my life hell. Nicole was by my side, day in and
day out. I truly love her for that.

4. **Outta sight, outta mind**. I do not have to tell you
that clinging to mementos, old photos, his Oral B
in your medicine cabinet . . . not healthy. I collect
everything in a relationship: every little present,
card, note, matchbook, photo, anything symbolizing
our relationship. What can I say? I'm sentimental. I
do it so if we get married, we have lots to look back
on and share. It's a nice thought—but it totally sucks
when I break up with a guy. I am surrounded by all
this shit that screams his name. If this is also your
problem, then my solution is simple: get rid of it.
Rip it, shred it, burn it, stomp on it, throw it into a
garbage bag and then pour marinara sauce on it. So
much for sentimental. And I highly recommend that
if you do this, you accompany it with a loud "Fuck
you, you son of a bitch!" for extra emphasis. The one
thing that really helped Snook get over the hump
was burning her ex's pics. It was a symbolic gesture,
but it also helped her rid her room of the evidence
that he ever was a part of her life. If you can't bear to
burn things (or can't bring yourself to be as violent
with disposing of them as I am), then at the very
least, put anything that triggers a memory of your ex

in a box in the basement where you don't have to see it every day.

5. **Figure out how the relationship got fucked up.** This was a big one for me, because it led me to learn from my mistakes and write my rules and now share them with you. Before I did this, I kept repeating the same stupid patterns over and over. Analyzing a failed relationship is a good thing, but I don't think you should do it right away; you need at least a few months to clear your head before you let thoughts of that asshole creep back in. When you feel strong and stable enough, sit down and do an autopsy. What were the issues that kept coming up between us? What could I never live with in a relationship again? What do I want/not want from the next man I am with? While you're doing this, try not to blame yourself or make yourself nuts obsessing. It is what it is; it was what it was. Just write it down and file it away for future reference.

6. **Let it go**. After getting my heart ripped out more than a few times, I have come to a conclusion: there is no good reason to hang on to heartache, hatred, or regret. All it does is make you miserable—not to mention fat, if you bury your emotions in a plate of spaghetti like most Guidos/Guidettes do. You took a chance and it didn't work out this time. Move the

fuck on. You better believe he is! There will be a next time, maybe even a next time after that. I am a big believer in "everything happens for a reason." If I hadn't been in so many fucked-up relationships, I would never be as strong as I am today. I've taken a lot of blows, true, but now it's almost impossible to knock me down. So my advice to you is this: do your bitching, moaning, crying, and hibernating . . . then pick your ass up, dust yourself off, and get on with your life.

RULE 31: IF YOU'RE KICKING HIS ASS TO THE CURB, DO IT WITH DIGNITY

It isn't always the dude who does the dumping—though that's what they'd have you believe. A lot of the time, it's the woman who ends it, and there are ways to go about that. Some are kind, some are sadistic. I guess it all depends on what dirty business went down between the two of you. I say, no matter how you decide to deliver the news, you should keep your wits about you and remember you want to walk away from this proud and strong. Do not allow him to push your buttons or blame you. Desperate guys say desperate things—remember that.

First off, you need to be sure you want to do this. Weigh the pros and cons. Is there any chance of salvaging the relationship? Do you want to? Was it a onetime offense that caused you to want to give him his walking papers, or has he been a repeat offender.

Be prepared for how he could react. In the case of The Guido, he later admitted to me that the day after I left, he had a breakdown in his apartment. He went downstairs and saw his empty living room. He realized the only thing I had left behind (accidentally) was Bella's dog bowl, and he hit the floor on his knees hysterically crying for hours. He finally realized I was the best thing he ever had, but the damage was done. I can't say I'm surprised by his reaction; nothing at this point surprises me. Some guys get angry, while others will beg you to reconsider and swear up and down they'll "be good." In the end, a girl's gotta stand her ground, no matter how hard he tries to change her mind.

Once you know what needs to be done, then I recommend doing it face-to-face. An e-mail, a letter, a text . . . that just screams, "I'm a fucking coward." You're better off sitting him down, looking him in the eyes, and telling him how you feel and why you think you two need to go your separate ways. If distance is an issue, then do the deed over the phone if you can't wait for a visit.

Keep it short, sweet, and to the point. "It's done" might even suffice. If he wants to know why, he's grasping at straws—he knows exactly what led up to this. But if you feel particularly generous, you could calmly explain how you feel and what caused you to feel this way. Who knows? Maybe he'll actually take notes and not do this to the next girl he dates. But you know my opinion on that: once a douchebag, always a douchebag. At least he'll be someone else's douchebag and not yours anymore.

RULE 32: REHEATED PASTA NEVER TASTES THE SAME

I don't care how great that plate of penne à la vodka was last Sunday night. When you serve it as leftovers on Tuesday, it just ain't as good. The same goes for relationships: if you rekindle your ex-files, do not expect things to be the way they were when you first were together. Sometimes, in a rare case, they're better. Because you've both done some growing and maturing and put time and space between you. But most of the time—and certainly in my case—all that's gonna come from getting back with him is heartburn.

There was this guy I dated post-Guido and pre-Mistake who we will call "Unimportant." We went back and forth for two years, and every time we would get back together, it was amazing right before it all went to shit again. I realize I dated him because he was super sexy and great in bed—that's about it. The moment I tried to make his ass into dating material, it was back to shit again. But I stupidly kept trying!

Let's be honest here: most breakups do not happen

out of nowhere and for no reason. You didn't just break up with him for the fun of it. But if you're thinking about getting back, then ask yourself this:

- Why do I want to get back with him?
- Do I want him because I don't have him?
- Have I had enough time to think this through?
- Have we resolved our past issues?
- Are there any reasons I shouldn't take him back?
- Is he the best person for me?
- What do my friends/family think of him?
- Are we willing to put the past behind us?
- Do we love each other and care about each other?
- Do I see a future with him?

If, after evaluating all of the above, you do decide to give it a go, I recommend never picking up where you left off (because it was most likely a fucking disaster area). Instead, treat it as a brand-new relationship. Think of yourself as a "virgin" all over again. If he wants to bang you, he has to go through the motions and do the work. He has to earn your trust—and the second time around is even tougher.

RULE 33: YOU GOTTA GET BACK IN THE GAME SOMETIME...

Unless you are planning on becoming a nun (I don't recommend it; the clothes are pretty unflattering), eventually you're going to have to hook up with another guy. If the very thought makes you wanna hurl . . . then you probably should hold off. But if you can hear his fave song on the dance floor and not start bawling like a baby, it's time.

That said, you don't have to jump into the ocean headfirst. You can stick your toe in the water and test the temperature. Just go out with girlfriends—no pressure, no expectations—and meet new people. It might feel creepy to be single again—I know it did for me at first. When I went through a breakup on the show, my roommates were concerned—and wondering if they should take cover from JWOWW on the loose! They wanted to know what my plans were. I said, "If I am single, we got a problem on our hands . . . I'll show my true side, my true, dirty, fucking filthy side!" And I meant it. There was something very liberating about being unattached again. You're always going to feel sad that things didn't work out the way you wanted them to. But don't let that hang over your head like a dark cloud. Don't let it hold you back from finding happiness—from finding someone who's worthy of you. Promise me—for your own good—you will not sit in your house for months on end pining away for that prick who done you wrong! You're too good for that, and you're letting opportunities pass you by.

DATE A DUDE FOR THE RIGHT REASONS

Not because he's so hot that your ex would be driven wild with jealousy; not because your apartment doesn't have heat and you need a warm body to snuggle up to; not because he is loaded and will buy you a Rolex. Make sure he measures up: he's kind, considerate, honest, and he treats you the way you deserve to be treated. Obviously, you have to be attracted to him, but make sure that's not the only reason you are with him. Remember that list of things you wanted/needed in a relationship? Stick to it. Do not compromise or let yourself be swayed by how big and tan his biceps are. If you do, I guarantee you will be back in the same boat again—cursing yourself out for being a sucker.

TAKE IT SLOW

There is no need to rush into a relationship right away. Enjoy just playing the field, or if you're with one guy, take the time to really get to know him. I say don't make any major decisions for at least seven weeks—that's just under two months, so it doesn't sound like an eternity. That means no claiming to be his "girlfriend" or saying the three big words, "I love you," even if you're dying to. He'll wait. If he cares for you and wants to be with you, he'll wait. If he bails because you're not in a hurry . . . I say, "Don't let the door hit you in the ass on the way out."

EXPLORE NEW OPTIONS

By this, I mean, don't be afraid to go out with a guy that doesn't fit the definition of "your type." Maybe your type is the type to screw with your head. And if that's the case, you need a new plan, man. You don't have to marry the guy, but maybe he'll be fun—and not a fucking loser—for a change? Take my girl Snooki in Miami: there were no Guidos to be found, so she expanded her horizons and decided to give a papi a try. It didn't work out, but it kept her entertained for a week or so. Nothing wrong with that. I say as long as you're attracted to him and have one or two things in common, give it a try. I love my Guidos, but occasionally, something else pretty catches my eye—like a rock-star singer of a band with chains and long hair . . . *yummm.* It's kind of like when you were a kid and your mom shoved vegetables in your face and you refused to eat them. She'd say, "How do you know you don't like it if you never try it?" Same applies here: take a bite.

STOP TALKING ABOUT YOUR EX

Seriously, stifle yourself. Your girlfriends are going to get sick of you obsessing (I already am!), and using his name five times in a sentence is not going to make him magically reappear in your life. This is also a huge turn-off for your new guy. If you have to, give him a code name; e.g.,"The Scumbag" or "Mr. Shithead." So if you simply MUST drop his name, it at least has a nice ring to it . . .

I really try not to bring up my exes to my current boyfriend, Perfection, but on occasion I have to or he asks. If that's the case, I keep it as short and negative as possible! I will bash the old boyfriends and explain why it didn't work, but keep it within the one-minute range. An hour-long tirade will make your man a little nervous anyway. As in, "I wonder if she'll trash me like this if we have problems down the road?" Or worse: he'll think *you're* the head case: "What kind of girl would allow herself to be in a relationship with an asshole like that?" It show's bad judgment and a lack of self-respect. So my advice to you: focus on the positive (the great guy you're with now) and not the negative (the bastard who made your life shit).

LET YOURSELF FALL IN LOVE

I know once you've been hurt, you think every guy you meet will play hit-and-run with your heart. But if you find a really nice guy, one who is doing his damnedest to prove to you that he's decent, don't allow your old baggage to sabotage what could be a good thing. Just because your last relationship ended up in the crapper doesn't mean this one will. Let your wall down, brick by brick, and allow him into your life.

Unfortunately, I dragged The Guido into every relationship I had that followed him. If any of the guys post-Guido did anything that resembled his MO, I would go for blood. I would automatically think they were cheating or lying and become this nasty-ass bitch who took no prisoners. For a while I was stuck in this vicious cycle: I'd date a guy, but after a week or so, I'd make a beeline for the exit. I had The Guido on the brain, and I couldn't allow myself to go through that kind of pain ever again. Pity any guy who asked me out—they had no idea what they were getting themselves into!

This was also the case when I met Perfection. I saw him a few times before we really got to know each other in Jersey. I knew I liked him, but I was off to Miami— and still dating The Mistake. After I broke up with The Mistake, it was a scary-shit time for me all over again, and I was afraid to like another guy. I kept trying to talk myself out of it and I made a pretty good argument:

1. I lived two hours from him. Long-distance dating never works.

2. There were only a few weeks left at the Shore—so how serious could it get?

3. I worried that he was only being "nice" because we were on TV. What if I suddenly discovered he's a total dick outside the range of the cameras, as so many of them are?

4. I knew hardly anything about his personal life. Did he have psycho exes? A good job? A nice house? Was he financially stable? A cheater? A liar? Using me?

I'll be honest, it wasn't looking too good for us in the relationship department. My fault, not his. A guy can't force you to trust him if you're dead set against it. Then one day I looked into his eyes and I caught myself smiling and thinking, "He makes me so happy, and that's all that matters . . . I need to take a chance." And so I did. Smartest decision I ever made. Sometimes love means taking a little leap of faith. You're never going to be 100 percent sure you won't get your heart broken—but you're also never 100 percent sure that you will. Weigh the odds and decide if it's a risk worth taking. In my case, I had a feeling that Perfection was just around the corner—and I wasn't about to let him get away.

I can't really tell you why I let an ex haunt me for so long—maybe because when I met him, I was just Jenni from upstate, so young, innocent, and naive, and eager to give everyone the benefit of the doubt. The Guido stole that from me, and I'll never be that person again. Even now, when I'm in a great relationship, I question and doubt and become hotheaded. That's my defense mechanism when I'm scared, and Perfection knows it. I love him even more for accepting me in this light. I've been working really hard on this, but I'm a woman scorned, and those scars, I warn you, take a very long time to heal.

THE BODY ISN'T EVEN COLD . . .

. . . and he's already taken up residence in some bitch's pants. Seeing your ex with someone else sucks, but you can at least take comfort in one fact: rebound relationships rarely work. That's because he's likely using this chick either to make you jealous or to fill his need to get banged on a regular basis. My advice: focus instead on your own social life. If he's dating, you have no reason to feel bad/ guilty about getting yourself a piece of hot ass ASAP and having fun.

But if you can't move on just yet, there's always payback. Revenge is not something I highly recommend (because it usually comes back to bite you in the ass), but you know I'm guilty of getting even once or twice! A perfect example: one night I found out The Guido had cheated on me and was actually about to go out and do it again. So I pulled a MacGyver—*Jersey Shore* style. I snatched his electronic BMW keys, wrapped them in a damp paper towel, and put them in the microwave, where I nuked those fuckers for five seconds. (Kids—do not try this at home!) It zapped the computer chip in them, so when he went to start his car . . . nada. Now, how you gonna cheat if you can't get anywhere? He spent hours trying to figure out what the hell was up with his precious car. I admit it: it gave me such pleasure to see him suffer. Sometimes a girl's gotta do what a girl's gotta do to get her head back in the game:

Show him what he's missing. Go for a makeover—lose weight, get a new haircut and color, hot clothes, even a boob job (well that might be a bit extreme!)—then walk by and watch his tongue hang out. Best revenge ever for me. I went to the gym and got in sick shape and The Guido noticed . . . boy, did he notice. But make sure you're doing it for yourself, not for him.

Date one of his best friends. Ouch—this is pretty evil. Because if you're lucky, your ex and his pal will wind up hating each other, or even better, pummeling each other at a club. Nothing makes a girl feel more appreciated than two men punching each other in the face over her! In terms of the friend you befriended . . . I don't suggest keeping the guy around long term, just long enough to see your ex cry in his beer. You don't want to let him get too attached so his feelings get hurt. Keep it cool and casual—except for the make-out session a few feet from where your former dirtbag is standing.

Be successful—and make sure he hears about it. Show him that being free of his sorry ass is the best thing that's ever happened to you. The Mistake thought he was God's gift to women, and he loved to tell me that I would never do better than him. Well, not only did I do better than him, I AM better than him—more together, more focused, more respected—not to mention happier. And I make headlines in magazines and newspapers. Read 'em and weep . . .

Humiliate his ass. Publicize all the shit he did to you. Don't name names, but he'll know it's him when you blab, blog, or write a book (heh, heh . . .) and dish the deets of your relationship hell. Even better if you have your own reality show! If you can't do any of the above, you can always throw a "Broke Up with His Ass" party and invite all his friends and yours to celebrate. For the e-vite, use a picture of the two of you. It shows you have a sense of humor, and being able to laugh about it will help you heal.

Dear JWOWW:

My boyfriend and I broke up after two years and he wants to stay friends. What do you think?

I think it's very, very tough—for the life of me, I will never understand how Demi Moore and Bruce Willis do it. I recommend it only if the following is true for you two:

The chemistry is dead. You feel nothing, not a tinge of lust or jealousy. This will come in handy when you see him with his tongue down some bitch's throat.

You're comfortable confiding in each other. You'd have no issue sharing details of your boob job or hearing about his latest conquest in graphic detail.

You parted on good terms. There was no screaming, crying, or death threats. You just simply decided you were better off un-coupled.

CHAPTER 6

STYLIN'

RULE 34: WHEN IT COMES TO STYLE,
YOU CALL THE SHOTS

Don't get me wrong—fashion magazines are a lot of fun to flip through and I enjoy getting ideas, eyeing hot clothes, and being inspired. But while I take what they say into consideration, I don't let anyone or anything dictate what I wear. My body/my clothes—that's how it goes. I don't give a shit if ripped acid-wash jeans are "out" not "in" this year. I like them and they work for me. I buy clothes and tweak them all the time—cutting and shredding tops and tees, bleaching jeans and ripping holes into them and splattering paint on them. So instead of buying a $200 pair of jeans because they are shredded and have a few paint marks on them, I buy a $25 pair and DIY. And I really don't give a flying fuck if someone ranks my dress as Worst of the Week. I know my style isn't for everyone, and that's okay. I like being the one and only JWOWW!

Fashion should make you feel good about yourself. It shouldn't be a shallow game of follow the leader, with everyone acting like a slave to the latest trends. I don't follow the trends; I prefer to set my own and I think everyone should embrace that attitude. Comb the racks, read the mags, then decide what looks you like and rock it any which way you want. For example, maybe the military look is in this year, but you wouldn't be caught dead in a jacket with shiny gold buttons and freakin' fringe on the shoulders. You would, however, consider a cute pair of khaki shorts, a white tank, and a camo baseball hat. Done deal.

Fashion is a way of expressing yourself, an opportunity to stand out from the crowd, not just blend in. Take a look on the runways—there are probably plenty of whacked-out couture looks no woman would be caught dead in (unless your name is Gaga). But that doesn't stop a fashion designer from putting it out there, from being creative and pushing the envelope. I don't say you should dress inappropriately, but I see nothing wrong with injecting your personality into what you wear. It's why I took a spin at designing my own line, JWOWW Couture—I loved the creativity of mixing fabric, color, and cut to create something entirely unique for the club scene. If I had to label my personal style, I would say it's "Sexy Sophisticated." Some critics have dubbed it "Stripper Chic"—and I can live with that. I've been called worse! Do I sometimes push the boundaries of taste? Guilty as charged. But I have a hell of a lot of fun doing it!

I should probably fess up that I didn't always look like this. I started out a fucking fashion emergency. When I was a teenager, I was all about four-wheeling, go-karting, snowmobiling, and martial arts—a huge tomboy. I loved getting dirty, and I was never into hair and makeup. In fact, I always wore my hair up along with wearing baggy sweats and sweaters. I just lived for comfort.

When I grew up and hit the club scene, I came into my own and figured out my style through trial and error. These days, it isn't one look I rock all the time; it's more about what mood I'm in. I was never into playing dress-up as a kid, so now's my chance! I love dressing sexy and showing off my cleavage, but then I also love wearing business suits or chains with ripped shirts. It really depends on how I wake up feeling. Some days I wanna be a princess, while other days I might be in the mood for something edgier—like rocker chick. I can pull off every look, and I like to think I'm a master of it. Guys *love* this, by the way—it's that element of surprise again, the stuff that keeps them guessing what you're made of.

How I dress on *Jersey Shore* is really only two sides of me. You get the hungover sweats and big tee side, and then there's the JWOWW out on the prowl: small shirts, ripped jeans, and skimpy dresses accessorized with chains, big hoops, towering heels. This is what I think of as "power prowl dressing." Nicole has her own style going, too—Guidette all the way, but with that playful Snooki spin. She rocks the whole animal-print look—which is something I would never feel comfortable pulling off—but on her, it's amazing. Very tiger on the hunt. Then there's Sam's look—cute short-shorts and simple black or white dresses—what I would call "Subtle Guidette." We all got our own style going on.

THE ELEMENTS OF GUIDO STYLE

....

Most Guidos—including the guys in my *Shore* house—are all talk, no action when it comes to fashion. They don't take many style risks; they travel in packs, so they tend to dress like their posse. In a nutshell: "It's T-shirt time!" It could get a little monotonous, except for the fact that these guys have sick bodies (so I will forgive the unoriginality). But occasionally, they do dress up for you in a nice button-down (buttoned way down!), khakis, footwear other than Converse. And that's pretty much when I lose all control . . .

GUIDO HAIR

"Gel or go home" is their motto. The style can be a
blowout, a fohawk, short and spiked, or buzzed into
a sleek fade. Guidos spend a lot of time on their hair,
both in the bathroom and at the barbershop. Pauly has
it down to a science—twenty-five minutes tops from
wash to dry to out the door. And his hair is legendary;
he's like the Farrah Fawcett of the Shore.

GUIDO TATTS

99.9 percent of Guidos have tattoos. Apparently,
you can't be a member of the team unless you're
sporting ink. Personally, I love men with tattoos,
especially sleeves and back done. It's like smushing
a work of art. Crosses, fire-breathing dragons, wild
animals, weapons, claws, wings . . . all incredibly sexy.
Your mother's name in a heart, your ex's portrait,
SpongeBob . . . not so much. Guidos also often sport
piercings: ears, nose, tongue, even below the belt. A
stud or small hoop here and there is hot; a chandelier
dangling from a guy's lower lip isn't.

GUIDO BODS

True Guidos are ripped out of their minds. My *Shore*
mates are prime examples. There is nothing—I repeat
NOTHING—like washboard abs and biceps bigger
than my head. Guidos wear their muscles like a trophy:
"I've won this for spending endless hours in the gym
busting my ass." I'm impressed!

GUIDO TANS

Guidos believe that when it comes to scoring, if you're pale, you fail. Maybe that's the reason Vin hit his stride in Season Two—the kid was rocking a serious tan. The bronze look can be achieved in numerous ways—from tanning beds, to spray-on, to baking on the beach. I don't care how they do it—just show me a golden-brown Guido god and I'm down for pretty much anything.

GUIDO OUTFITS

Once you've put all of the above together, you got half the Guido. The clothes make the man. Most of them rock jeans by Seven or True Religion—the upscale denims that emphasize two key Guido selling points: the butt cheeks and the package. They top that off with cutoff-sleeve shirts, wife beaters, or tight guinea tees. Shirts are almost always blinged out—the very best Ed Hardy, Armani Exchange, or Affliction has to offer. Guidos are all about name brands—and that goes for accessories as well. Watches, sunglasses, sneaks—they better all be status. Many of them also adorn their perfect pecs with glittering crosses and chains—kind of like decking out a Christmas tree. Fucking fa-la-la-la-la! Everything a Guido wears is very clean and fresh to death: clothes are crisp with not a wrinkle in them; the shoes are polished with not one smudge mark; the jewelry shining. It's a beautiful package to unwrap.

RULE 35: YOU CAN'T GO WRONG WITH CLEAVAGE

Why? Because the mere sight of The Girls out in the open turns men to Jell-O. Maybe it reminds them of their first meal. Maybe a glimpse of what you're offering helps them fantasize what a night with you would be like. I can't explain it, but I do know that boobs hypnotize the opposite sex. I've walked into a club and had guys' eyes lock on my rack like heat-seeking missiles.

If you've ever seen me, you know I am all about making the "breast-dressed" lists. I'm so used to wearing low-cut tops that when the boss at Lecca-Lecca Gelato in South Beach asked me to put on a big T-shirt, I felt like my boobs were choking to death. I do think there is a time and a place to be "tit-illating." You probably wanna rein them in at your workplace (unless you're a waitress at Hooters or a pole dancer) and air them out when you're partying or on a date. Just let me give you fair warning: men are pretty simpleminded. You may be sporting The Ladies to show you're a powerful, sexy, confident woman, but they're not necessarily going to get that message. To them, tits and ass is tits and ass. All they're probably thinking is, "How do I get me some of that?" So be careful how much of your assets you air in public. You want to look sexy, not slutty. Sometimes I see chicks who would probably be more covered up wearing two Band-Aids. I don't care how proud you are of your twins, if your cup runneth over . . . it's too much.

I also want to emphasize that you don't need boobs the size of mine to show cleavage. Thank God for the invention of the Wonderbra. If a woman is confident in her body—no matter what size or shape it is—then I say, "Rock it, sister." And if you're not . . . there are plenty of padded bras out there and plastic surgeons that can work miracles. I wanted boobs that defied gravity, and boy, did I get them! I was about the same size but I wanted a more dramatic look, so I bought them for myself for my twenty-first birthday. I couldn't be more happy with them—and I have never heard a man complain.

RULE 36: NEVER WEAR A GRANNY ON YOUR FANNY

Guys—as much as they would like to—do not have X-ray vision. So unless you're down to get naked, they probably have no idea what you're wearing beneath your smokin'-hot outfit. That is not, however, an excuse to go out in undies that look like they belong to your eighty-year-old nonna. You know what I'm talking about: beige, white, droopy drawers. Ones with holes or stains, or worse, days of the week written on them. Imagine a man's horror if he's letting his fingers do the walking and he runs into a Hanes hipster! I beg you: invest a few bucks in some seductive skivvies. They are worth every cent and will practically wind up paying for themselves when you're getting laid. Personally, I like Frederick's of Hollywood. Their bras are full-on sexy, and they actually fit me. I also like Victoria's Secret, but they're usually not made for my size boobs. Whatever brand you buy, think lace, color, and *feel*. Run your hands over it—would it give a guy a hard-on or a heart attack? Satin, silk, see-through—all A-plus in my book. Nothing that even vaguely resembles a sports bra should be on your body unless you're hitting a treadmill. All you need is to get caught in my *Shore* house in an ugly pair of drawers! Guido roommates don't quite grasp the meaning of the word "privacy," so if they barge in on you half naked, and if you're in anything other than a thong or booty shorts . . . you're toast. The whole house will hear about it.

But even if you don't have an audience, you can get creative. Try out a G-string, a bustier, a merry widow, a garter . . . even crotchless. And if you have no idea what any of those are . . . oh, baby, you got some homework to do! Have fun with it and start a collection. Just knowing that you're wearing something secretly sexy will boost your confidence and make you feel desirable. Just one word to the wise: beware The Britney. Even if you don't have a clean pair, do not go to a club bare. After a couple Long Island iced teas, you might be doing the "Jersey Turnpike" on the dance floor and accidentally flash everyone the goods. Imagine that as someone's iPhone screen saver!

RULE 37: YOU DON'T NEED SOME FANCY GUY'S NAME ON YOUR ASS

By this, I mean don't be a slave to name brands. A lot of girls will only buy an outfit if it has a fancy designer label attached to it. That's fucking ridiculous. Guidos, as I mentioned, are famously brand-conscious, but that's only for themselves. They generally don't give a shit what designer a girl is wearing—they can't tell the difference. You think a guy is checking out the name on your jeans back pocket . . . or how sexy your ass looks? I rest my case.

Always buy the clothes that fit you the best, regardless of who makes them. My favorite stores to shop in are Affliction, Bebe, Caché, Guess, Armani Exchange, Le Château, Steve Madden, and Express. I find them all reasonably priced and the clothes are quality and cool. Occasionally I'll pick up a designer look I really love—like a Michael Kors—but it truly pains me to overspend on clothing. I'm not about the labels; I could buy a $5 shirt from one store or a $150 shirt at another. The only thing that matters to me is how it looks on me. My maximum is $300 on a bag, and I stick to it. If a more expensive one is on sale or at a thrift or vintage store, be my guest. But shelling out thousands for a scrap of fabric or a bag that has some letters stamped all over it? I can think of a dozen better things to spend that money on— like say a house share next summer.

I also don't recommend buying a fake designer anything. You may not be able to tell the difference, but you bet your ass somebody will, and they'll call you out on it—especially if you're trying to pass it off as authentic. My girls and I love to make fun of some bitch rocking a knockoff Louis Vuitton at the club (gee, the "IU" instead of "LV" initials weren't too much of a giveaway, were they?). She's putting on airs, acting like her shit don't stink—and her bag cost twenty bucks off the street in Chinatown. If you can't afford the real thing, then go for Guess. It's much cooler to keep it real.

WORK TO PARTY IN UNDER TEN

HOW TO GO FROM CASUAL TO CLUB-READY IN TEN MINUTES OR LESS

If you're leaving the office and going straight to a club, I suggest prepping in the morning—shower, blow out, and iron/curl your hair, moisturize and do your makeup (see Chapter 8 for beauty how-tos). Then it's all about the quick change:

STEP 1: Wear jeans to work (if you're allowed), topped with a nice sweater, blouse, or a cami and blazer. This will be your look till checkout time . . .

STEP 2: Pack a pair of heels and a sexy shirt and put them on with the jeans when it's time to party.

STEP 3: Add accessories: some big, colorful hoop earrings, an armful of bangles, belt chains. I'm into grungy jewelry that has skulls and crosses on them, and I score a lot of great pieces at Hot Topic. They're also awesome for body jewelry if that's your thing—everything from tongue studs to belly barbells. The boss doesn't have to know what's hiding under your conservative suit!

STEP 4: If you're a fan of clip-on hair extensions like I am, it takes about five minutes to weave them into your 'do. Choose ones that match your shade if you want to be subtle and just pump up the volume; go with an opposite hue if you want to be edgier (black if you're a blond; blond if you're a brunette).

STEP 5: Finish with your game face (see Chapter 8), then pack some makeup (for touch-ups) in a small bag that won't weigh you down on the dance floor. You're good to go!

RULE 38: YOUR CLOTHES SHOULD RIDE YOUR CURVES

If you're trying to attract a man, then your clothes need to showcase your body in a sexy, "See something you like?" sort of way. A lot of ladies make a huge mistake buying too big. You're covering up and camouflaging your best assets instead of flaunting them. It may be more comfortable to go with something flowy rather than a tight dress, but billowy fabric will actually make you look fatter than you are. I'm not saying squeeze yourself into a dress so you look like an Italian sausage; I'm just saying anything you wear should *fit*. If it doesn't, spend the $30 to get it tailored. And if you're lacking in the curves department, no worries: they even make panties these days that come with a little extra fill where you need it. Like a padded bra for your ass!

RULE 39: BASIC BLACK IS BORING

I will rock an LBD when the occasion calls for something classy; black is universally flattering and forgiving—not to mention the sexy shade of night. But I urge you to color your world when you go clubbing. Hot pink, ruby red, bright yellow—all these shades will look fucking hot against tanned, sweaty skin. Same goes for loud prints (did someone say "Snooki"?) and heels in hot shades. I love to use color to call attention to myself—

basically, wherever you wear a bright shade, a guy's eye will go to. Great legs? Wear bubble-gum-pink stilettos. Proud of your double Ds? Don a red top to signal "Hey, dude, over here!" You can fucking wear the colors of the Italian flag if you feel like it—just OWN IT. You have to wear color with confidence. You can't court the spotlight then cower in the corner. When I walk into a room in a red dress, I feel like I'm on fire. A hot hue does wonders for your confidence and charisma.

But there are some colors I would tell you to avoid on the scene. For example, you do not want to be dressed in white or cream at a crowded club. What if someone spills, slobbers, steps on you? Suddenly your white-hot skirt is covered in some dick's rum and Coke. Your night is ruined. I'd also be wary of wearing dark colors head to toe—like black or brown—if you're going to a dimly lit lounge. No one will notice you. At the very least, add a few bright flashy accessories so they can see you coming.

RULE 40: WHAT YOU SHOULD WEAR...

AT THE CLUB

Make sure you show your hips, ass, and boobs in a sexy way; your clothes should cling to your body, giving guys a guide to what's lurking underneath. Accentuate the look with stilettos, bracelets, rings and earrings, and a clutch, all in the same color family so you look pulled together—not trashy.

AT THE BAR

If you're going out for casual drinks, then tone it down a notch. Wear tight jeans, tight shirt, heels, or high-heeled boots. Keep the accessories minimal: stick to earrings and a cute ring. And make sure whatever you wear isn't so tight you can't sit and bend. If you're going to be on a bar stool, you wanna be able to breathe!

AT THE LOUNGE

These places are a little more classy. You can never go wrong in a sexy black cocktail dress with a few glitzy accessories—like gold hoops, some bangles, and open-toe or sling-back stilettos.

ON A FIRST DATE

Always show the goods, but not too much. Leave something to the imagination. Tight dress all the way, but don't overdo the accessories or the makeup. You want to dress to impress . . . not to excess.

MEETING HIS FAMIGLIA

Cover up! Nice sweater, jeans, and boots will work in fall and winter. If it's the hot-ass summer, wear a cute sundress that doesn't showcase your tits. Do not, I repeat, do not reveal shit . . . you never know what could happen.

Do I have to remind you how Vinny's uncle Nino was hanging all over us girls in the hot tub? Fucking out of control!

AT THE BEACH

A bathing suit that shows off your figure in a flattering, sexy way. If you're comfortable in an itty-bitty string bikini, go for it. My Snooks rocks a monokini to perfection! Add a cute hat and sunglasses and wear chunky sandals. They may suck really bad in the sand, but they make your legs look miles longer.

WHEN YOU'RE DTF

Make sure your bra and panties match. Basically, nothing else matters because you're going to wind up hanging whatever outfit you choose over his bedpost. But if you're trying to bait a boy for the night, then pull out all the stops: show skin and cleavage, as much as you can get away with without getting arrested.

Dear JWOWW:

I'm about forty pounds overweight and want to look hot when I go out. Any suggestions on what I should wear?

My answer to this is simple: anything that makes you feel good. I don't think you need to be a certain size to be sexy. Sexy means different things to different people. Maybe you don't want to show so much skin—that's cool. Play up your best body parts, whether it's double Ds, a bootylicious butt, or hot legs. The one thing I beg you: do not cover yourself up in some fuckin' tent. If you're fortunate enough to be curvy in all the right places, find a flattering dress and emphasize your waist. There are also tons of plus-size stores and websites that specialize in club clothes and lingerie. You can be a voluptuous vixen!

CHAPTER 7

BODY

RULE 41: IF A GUY'S GONNA STARE AT YOUR BOOBS
AND ASS, THEY BETTER LOOK DECENT

I hate to break it to you: the first thing a guy notices about you is not your sparkling personality. It's your body. He's checking you out, and that's what makes the strongest first impression. In a split second, his mind forms an opinion: "Damn, she's hot!" or "Damn, she's not!" You might win him over after that with your brains, beautiful face and hair, and great sense of humor, but I promise you, he notices right off the bat if you are rocking rock-hard arms or carrying around a little junk in the trunk.

Obviously, I am not a stick figure. In high school, I was an average weight but I was a tomboy so being athletic kept me in shape. When I shot Season 1 of *Jersey Shore*, I started out in great shape, but between drinking, sleeping, and being very sick with an upper respiratory infection . . . I gained probably eight pounds by the time I got home. Since Miami, I've lost about ten pounds. I am 5'7" and my weight ranges from 128 to 135 pounds.

I believe a woman should look like a woman; she should have dangerous curves and be healthy-looking, not emaciated. I do not buy into the whole "Hollywood image" of what is attractive, and you will not catch me strutting down some red carpet with my bones sticking out of my back. That is just fucking disgusting! I am not impressed by a waif who looks like a sudden gust of wind would knock her over. I wanna hold that bitch down and force-feed her a plate of penne à la vodka! I like to eat. I like loaded fries, chicken fingers, and chocolate. I cannot imagine passing up an eight-course Italian feast made by Vinny's mama Paula. That's the secret of every Guido/Guidette (at least the ones who are in amazing shape). We indulge in the four basic food groups (pasta, bread, cheese, and booze), but we work it off in the gym the next day.

I do not want any woman or girl to read this rule and think I'm telling you to give yourself an eating disorder to get a man. That's bullshit. As I said before, the guys I know prefer a little meat on the bones. Healthy means a good weight for your height, a normal body mass index. If you don't know what that means, then ask your doctor or look it up. Don't let a number on the scale, a photo in a magazine, or even your own image in the mirror dictate if you're the right weight. Starvation is fucking stupid. Your body will hate you for it, and your metabolism will slow down to a snail's pace. You're like a machine; you need fuel to function. If you don't eat, you'll break down. Same goes for exercise: I know some girls who spend hours at the gym, obsessively sweating off every calorie. All you're doing is hurting yourself. No Guido wants to be banging a skeleton—he wants a little cushion for the pushin'!

My change in diet and exercise has nothing to do with being a "celebrity" or even wanting a boyfriend. It had to do with me caring enough about myself (finally!) to take care of myself. It had to do with me feeling strong—as much mentally as physically. I was always athletic and into sports, but when I was nineteen, I started running 3.5 miles a day and was "shredded." When I turned twenty-one, I got into the Guidette lifestyle and club scene and started to hit the gym harder. Of course, I loved it when guys would stare and try to pick me up. Total rush! But I also knew that being fit was sending a positive message: I give a shit about my health. I give a shit about how I look. My head is in the right place and my body is a reflection of that.

So yes, I'm an advocate of working out, but I'm also a realist. My weight fluctuates a lot, especially when I go to the Shore. When a girl combines a lax schedule with drinking and late-night eating, of course she is going to gain weight. If I didn't work out—and I lived like this year-round—my ass would probably be the size of Giants Stadium! But I try to make up for it when our season is done shooting.

Currently, I am all about getting into shape and I have my boyfriend to thank for it. He's Mr. Perfect—or as close as one can get to it—physically. And seeing how in shape he is makes me want to get in the best shape I can be in. I love how he thinks I'm the most gorgeous girl in the world, and I want him to continue thinking that for years to come.

At this point in my life, I want to be healthy; I want to be full of energy and alert and on top of my game. I want to walk into a meeting with business types or reporters and feel confident, strong, sexy. Exercise does that for me. Yeah, I still love it when I turn heads at the club. But I'm also thinking about the future. I'm not a kid anymore! I'm not nineteen, and I gotta think how I'm gonna feel ten years from now when I'm pushing thirty-five. Gravity is a real bitch.

RULE 42: MAKE TIME FOR EXERCISE IN YOUR LIFE—EVEN IF IT KILLS YOU

There are mornings when I am hungover and the last thing I feel like doing is fifty squats with my trainer. It sucks. I fucking want to rip his head off. But I do it. Why? Because it's part of my life. I wouldn't skip a day of brushing my teeth or hit the beach without shaving my pits. Same principle: it's just something I need to do. I try to encourage all my girls at the Shore to join me, but it has to be a passion for people. It will never last with anyone who doesn't have the drive to get up and go—and I am not about to be anyone's nagging mother, dragging her ass out of bed. The guys, however, really respect me for doing this. They notice my body is changing and I'm getting smaller and more toned. I lost almost ten pounds leaving the Jersey Shore after the summer of 2010, which is good news, since the camera really does add ten pounds. Fans are usually shocked to see me in person because I look so much smaller! But honestly, it's been only about ten pounds. Where I've really made the difference is in definition and tone. No more Jell-O!

On good days, maybe I'll work out longer or harder. But five days out of seven, I do something, anything, to get my body moving and my heart pumping. I try to do twenty-five to thirty-five minutes of cardio a day, five days a week. And after cardio, I pick one or two body parts to work out. I set it up like this:

Day 1: Shoulders: five exercises, each three sets of fifteen reps.
Abdominals: three exercises.
Butt: three exercises.

Day 2: Triceps and biceps: five exercises, each three sets of fifteen reps.
Abdominals: two exercises.

Day 3: Legs: ten exercises, three sets of fifteen reps.
Abdominals: three exercises.

Day 4: Back: five exercises, each three sets of fifteen reps.
Abdominals: two exercises.

Day 5: Total body: two exercises, each body part. (It's a long day!)

My trainer helped me put together this exercise plan (I'm also going to be releasing an exercise DVD in the next few months) that focuses on the parts a woman wants to perfect: the butt, boobs, abs, legs, arms, shoulders, and back. I suggest starting off slow if you've never done an exercise program before. Check with your doctor first, and maybe even sign up for some training sessions to make sure your form is right so you don't hurt yourself. Do some kind of cardio for at least twenty minutes a day, building up to thirty. This can be running, jogging, walking. Flipping channels on the remote doesn't count, ladies. Sex, however, does!

FOR LEAN LEGS

Exercise 1: Squats with chair

1. Stand in front of a chair (with your back to the seat of the chair), with feet about hip- or shoulder-width apart.

2. Squeeze your abs and keep them as tight as you can as you bend your knees and slowly squat toward the chair.

3. Keep your knees behind your toes as you sit down on the chair for a few seconds.

4. Now contract your butt and hamstrings to lift up out of the chair and begin extending your legs until you're back to standing position.

5. Repeat this for one to three sets of ten repetitions. If you really want to feel the burn, squat down until you're just hovering over the chair, but don't sit your ass down.

Exercise 2: Squats with dumbbell

1. Stand with feet hip- or shoulder-width apart.

2. Hold dumbbells in each hand just outside the thighs or with arms bent above the shoulders. If you're just

starting out, go for lighter weights (one to three pounds). If you want to amp it up, choose five to eight pounds.

3. Bend the knees and lower your body into a squat. Stop when your knees are at a ninety-degree angle.

4. Squeeze your butt and leg muscles while keeping your upper body strong.

5. Slowly stand back up without locking the knees and repeat for one to three sets of ten repetitions. Always keep the knees in line with the toes!

Exercise 3: Standing calf raise
1. Stand on the floor and hold on to a bar or wall for balance.

2. Lift up onto your toes as high as you can, squeezing the calves.

3. Lower and repeat for sixteen reps.

Exercise 4: Walking lunges
1. Hold a weight in your right hand, arm straight up over your head. Choose a lighter weight (one to three pounds) for beginners; five to eight if you want a challenge.

2. Step back with the right foot into a lunge, taking the knee all the way to the floor.

3. Now take the left leg back, knee to the floor while still holding the weight up. You should be kneeling with the right hand up in the air.

4. Step forward with the right foot and then the left to standing position.

5. Repeat for eight reps and then switch the weight to the other hand and do the move starting with the left leg for eight more reps.

Exercise 5: Inner thigh squeeze

1. Lie down on the floor (or on an exercise mat if it's more comfy) and lift your legs off the floor, placing an exercise ball (or some other type of ball) between your knees/shins.

2. Squeeze the ball lightly to keep it from dropping and put you hands on the floor for more support.

3. Slowly squeeze the ball, contracting your inner thighs.

4. Release just slightly, keeping some tension on the ball.

5. Repeat for one to three sets of ten to fifteen reps.

SO YOU LOOK AS GOOD GOING AS YOU DO COMING . . .

Exercise 1: Back extension

1. Lie facedown on a mat and place your hands behind your head (if this is too tough, you can also keep them flat out in front of you in a "Superman" pose).

2. Squeeze your abs and keep them contracted throughout the exercise.

3. Squeeze your back, lifting your chest a few inches off the floor.

4. Lower and repeat for one to three sets of ten reps total. To add intensity, you can also lift the legs off the floor at the same time.

Exercise 2: Shoulder press

1. Begin standing or sitting with a light weight (one to three pounds) in your right hand.

2. Bend your elbow and bring the weight up so that it's just next to your right ear.

3. Keep your abs engaged to stabilize your body as you press the weight to your head.

4. Lower back down and repeat for one to three sets of ten reps.

5. Repeat the exercise with the left arm.

Exercise 3: Overhead barbell press

NOTE: If you're using a heavier weight (ten or more pounds), you might want to sit on a chair or bench that has back support.

1. Using a medium barbell (eight to ten pounds), hold bar with hands a little wider than shoulder width apart.

2. Bring the bar up to forehead level, elbows bent.

3. Slowly straighten your elbows and press the weight overhead without arching your back. Keep your abs tight and don't lock your elbows at the top of the movement.

4. Exhale and lower back to start.

5. Repeat for two to three sets of ten to fifteen repetitions, with a twenty- to thirty-second rest between sets.

FOR ARMS THAT DON'T JIGGLE

Exercise 1: Triceps kickback

1. Start by standing and holding a medium weight (eight to ten pounds) in both hands and bend over until your torso is at a forty-five-degree angle to the floor. Bend the knees if needed and keep the abs engaged to protect the lower back.

2. Begin the movement by bending the arms and pulling the elbows up to torso level.

3. Hold that position, then straighten your arms out behind you, squeezing the triceps muscles. At the end of the movement, your arms should extend along the body, palms facing each other.

4. Bend the arms back to starting position and repeat for ten reps. Try not to swing the arms to get the weight up. You can also do this exercise one arm at a time if you're using heavier weights or need more support for the lower back.

Exercise 2: One-arm triceps push-ups
1. Lie on your right side with your knees bent and your hips stacked.

2. Wrap your bottom arm around your waist and place your left hand on the floor in front of you. Your fingers should point toward the right.

3. Contract your triceps to push your body up and off the floor, straightening your left arm as much as you can without locking the elbow.

4. Lower a few inches and continue pushing up and down for eight to ten reps before switching sides.

Exercise 3: Skull crushers
1. Lie on the floor or a bench and hold a light-to-medium barbell (three to ten pounds) with your hands close together, about shoulder width apart.

2. Extend the arms straight up over your chest, palms face out and thumbs wrapped around so that they're next to the fingers.

3. Bend your elbows and lower the weight down to a few inches above your forehead.

4. Squeeze the triceps to straighten your arms without locking the joints.

5. Repeat for one to three sets of ten to sixteen reps.

Exercise 4: Hammer curls

1. Stand with feet about hip-width apart, abs engaged as you hold light-to-medium dumbbells (three to ten pounds) in front of your thighs.

2. Turn your hands so that the palms face each other, and squeeze the biceps to curl the weights toward your shoulders.

3. Keep your elbows stationary and only bring the weight as high as you can without moving your elbows.

4. Slowly lower the weights, keeping a slight bend in the elbows at the bottom, careful not to lock the joints.

5. Repeat for one to three sets of ten to fifteen reps.

Exercise 5: Concentration curl

1. Sit or kneel and hold a light dumbbell (one to five pounds) in your right hand.

2. Bend forward, keeping your abs engaged, and prop your right elbow against the inside of your right thigh.

3. Contract the biceps and curl your hand toward your shoulder without moving your elbow. You don't have to touch your shoulder.

4. Lower all the way down (keep a very slight bend in the elbow to keep tension in the biceps) and repeat for one to three sets of ten reps on each side.

FOR GRAVITY-DEFYING BOOBS

Exercise 1: Chest fly with dumbbells

1. Lie on the floor or on a workout bench. Hold light-to-medium weights (three to ten pounds) over the chest with your palms facing each other.

2. Keeping your elbows slightly bent, lower your arms out to the sides and down until they're level with your chest.

3. Keep your elbows in a fixed position and be sure not to lower the weights too low.

4. Squeeze your chest muscles to bring your arms back up as though you're hugging a tree.

5. Repeat for one to three sets of ten to fifteeen reps.

Exercise 2: Modified push-ups

1. Start on all fours with hands a bit wider than your shoulders.

2. Walk your knees back a bit in order to lean your weight on your hands and flatten your back.

3. Pull your abs in and, keeping back straight, bend your elbows and lower your body toward the floor until your elbows are at ninety-degree angles.

4. Push back up and repeat for one to three sets of ten to fifteen reps. Avoid sticking your ass up in the air!

Exercise 3: Chest press with resistance bands

1. Wrap the band around something stable behind you (a doorknob of a shut door usually works) and hold the handles in both hands so that the bands run along the inside of your arms.

2. Position yourself far enough away (either sitting or standing) so that you have tension on the bands.

3. Begin the movement with your arms bent, palms facing down. Squeeze chest and press arms out in front of you, keeping the band stable. Do not lock your elbows or let them go too far back as you bring the arms in. This could strain the shoulders, and you want to keep all the work in the chest.

4. Repeat for one to three sets of ten reps.

FOR ABS THAT WOULD MAKE EVEN THE SITUATION JEALOUS

Exercise 1: The bicycle

1. Lie on the floor and lace your fingers behind your head.

2. Bring your knees in toward the chest and lift your shoulder blades off the floor without pulling on your neck.

3. Straighten your left leg out while simultaneously turning your upper body to the right, taking your left elbow toward your right knee.

4. Switch sides, bringing your right elbow toward your left knee.

5. Continue alternating sides, "pedaling" for one to three sets of ten to fifteen reps.

Exercise 2: Vertical leg crunch

1. Lie on the floor and extend your legs straight up with knees crossed.

2. Place your hands flat on the floor for support.

3. Contract your abs to lift your shoulder blades off the floor, as though you're reaching your chest toward your feet.

4. Keep your legs in a fixed position and imagine bringing your belly button toward your spine at the top of the movement.

5. Lower and repeat for one to three sets of ten to fifteen reps.

Exercise 3: Exercise-ball crunch

1. Lie on the ball, positioning it under your lower back.

2. Cross your arms over your chest or behind your head if you need more support.

3. Contract your abs to lift your torso off the ball, pulling the bottom of your rib cage down toward your hips.

4. As you curl up, keep the ball stable; it shouldn't roll!

5. Lower your back down, feeling a stretch in the abs, and repeat for one to three sets of ten to fifteen reps.

FOR A BOOTYLICIOUS BUTT

Exercise 1: Hip extensions on all fours

1. On hands and knees, keep your abs tight as you lift one leg up, knee at a ninety-degree angle.

2. Keep lifting the leg until the bottom of your foot faces the ceiling and your hip, thigh, and knee are all in alignment and parallel to the floor.

3. Don't arch your back and keep your neck straight.

4. Lower your leg back down and repeat for all reps before switching sides.

5. Add ankle weights for more intensity and do one to three sets of ten to fifteen reps.

Exercise 2: Lunges
1. Stand with feet about three feet apart. You want both knees to be at about ninety-degree angles at the bottom of the movement, so adjust accordingly.

2. Hold a light weight (one to five pounds) in each hand for added intensity.

3. Bend your knees and lower your back knee toward the floor, keeping the front heel down with the knee directly over the center of the foot.

4. Keep your torso straight and your abs in as you push through the front heel and back to starting position. Don't lock your knees at the top of the movement.

5. Perform one to three sets of ten to fifteen reps.

Exercise 3: Step-ups
1. Stand behind a fifteen-inch platform or step, with light weights (one to five pounds) in both hands.

2. Place your right foot on the step, transferring your weight to the heel, and come up onto the step. Concentrate on using only the right leg, keeping the left leg active only for balance.

3. Slowly step back down and repeat all reps on the right leg before switching to the left.

4. Perform one to three sets of ten to fifteen reps.

RULE 43: IF ALL YOU EAT IS GARBAGE, YOU'LL FEEL LIKE GARBAGE

You know that old saying, "You are what you eat?" I'd hate to be a fucking Frito-Lay. Or a Ring Ding . . . or a pint of Chubby Hubby. The image of that helps keep me on track. I know that a person can't survive on junk alone (tempting as it is when our *Shore* house fridge is filled with all sorts of shit). But like everyone else, I have my good days and my bad days. A good day is when I make sure I eat plenty of greens, fruits, and proteins. A bad day is when I was out all night tossing back drinks and shoveling in handfuls of bar mix. It happens. I don't beat myself up about it. I'll do better tomorrow. The way I see it, it's about striking a balance.

I also hate the word "diet." For starters, it makes me feel like a big fat fucking failure to be on one. Like I need to be restricting what I'm eating because I screwed up and am nearing hippo proportions. So instead, I am down for a "healthy eating plan"—a reward instead of a punishment! Try to wrap your brain around that: for every piece of crap you eliminate from your plan, there are about a dozen better choices you can actually add. Suddenly you have lots of options—not limitations. When you see it from that perspective, it's much easier to say good-bye to your daily trip to Dunkin' Donuts. I also believe eating healthy is empowering—it's about making choices for yourself. When you grab an apple instead of a Snickers, you're in control—you are one powerful bitch! I feel really good when I reach for something I know won't go to my ass . . .

JWOWW'S HEALTHY EATING PLAN

Breakfast
Option 1: Protein shake
Option 2: Bowl of Smart Start cereal with skim milk, fruit
Option 3: Egg-white omelet with broccoli, tomato, and onion (or your veggie of choice)

Lunch
Option 1: Chicken Caesar salad
Option 2: Low-sodium chicken soup (two-hundred-calorie can)
Option 3: Turkey sandwich: turkey, tomato, lettuce on wheat (no mayo)

Dinner
Option 1: Sashimi (four pieces of salmon, four pieces white tuna) and miso soup
Option 2: Grilled chicken, brown rice, grilled asparagus
Option 3: Turkey meatballs, steamed brown rice, cucumber salad

Snacks

Low-fat granola bar

Two hundred-calorie pack snacks

    (pretzels, crackers, popcorn, etc.)

Fresh fruit

String cheese

Handful of almonds

RULE 44: IT'S OKAY TO CHEAT...
ON YOUR DIET, THAT IS

A once-a-week cheat day isn't going to screw up your fitness plan. In fact, it will probably help you stick to it better, since you won't be obsessed over all the food you "can't" eat. I never say never; there is nothing (unless you have a serious health problem) that you can't eat. Sugar, fried food, alcohol . . . everything is okay in moderation. If you totally deprive yourself, I guarantee you will wind up dreaming of cannolis covered in chocolate. I don't know about you, but that isn't the kind of fantasy I want to be having in bed.

Grant yourself one day a week to have whatever you fucking feel like. I see it as the perfect opportunity to have a big Sunday dinner. I love to cook Italian, so once a week, my boyfriend and I stay home and eat in. I'll either put up some pasta, or we will order something greasy and delicious—like pizza, Japanese, cheese fries. I try not to be a pig about it; I keep the portions small, but I have a taste of anything and everything. For dessert, we'll rent a movie, pop popcorn, and feed each other "healthy" sundaes: sugar-free vanilla ice cream, fat-free brownies, sugar-free chocolate syrup, light whipped cream. The next day, it's back to being good. I make sure to double up on cardio and eat plenty of protein and fiber and drink lots of water to make up for all the crap I enjoyed over the weekend. I feel like I can enjoy food this way—not be afraid of it.

ADDED INCENTIVE: THE GYM IS GUIDO CENTRAL!

Do I even need to remind you that Guidos go to the gym more religiously than they go to church? No matter what time of day or night you hit it, they're there. Pumping. Sweating. Groaning. Flexing and stretching and bending over . . . oh, my. Honestly . . . it's better than watching the porn channel on cable. I say go for the sheer entertainment value; the fact that you'll get in great shape at the same time is icing on the cake. Who needs to watch TV on the elliptical when you have a front-row seat to sexy juice monkeys on parade?

Don't even leave it up to chance: ask the front desk when most of the bodybuilders work out. Set your alarm clock. And don't be shy if you see something you like. If I'm into a guy at the gym, I find something I can use nearby him to work out on, and then flash him a cute smile. If he smiles back, I take that as an opener but don't do anything the first day. The next time I see him, I ask him to help me with a machine, either change the weights or show me how to do it correctly. Men love a damsel in distress—and Guidos love to show what experts they are at weight training. If he takes the bait, then feel free to flirt some more for a few days before slipping him your number. A match made over muscles—what could be more romantic?

Dear JWOWW,

I have a hot date Saturday night. It's Monday, and I need to lose a few pounds fast. What can I do?

I suggest no sugar or carbs all week (stick to veggies and salad) and drink lots of water with lemon. You'll drop a few pounds in water weight—but be warned, it won't last!

CHAPTER 8

BEAUTY

Once the bod is looking hot, and the outfit accentuates your tits and assets, it's time to do your 'do and makeup. Guidettes are a rare breed of beauty. I know this look isn't for everyone (it takes a really confident bitch to wear a pouf!), but I urge you to give it a try, just once. It's much more than the makeup, the tan, or the big hair—it's about the attitude. Guidettes don't give a fuck. Why? Because we *know* we're hot.

THE ELEMENTS OF GUIDETTE BEAUTY

....

The tan. Guidettes wear their bronzed skin like a coat of armor. You want to go for a golden brown, as opposed to Oompa-Loompa orange.

The nails. An acrylic French mani is a must. No chips or smudges; your fingers should be flawless. Until you bust one scratching some bitch's eyes out. Of course, I don't do the standard mani. Fuck, no, I'm JWOWW. Instead of white, my tips are black, grey, red . . . it all depends on my mood that week. Plus, I get sparkles with a gel top. Flawless!

The hair. Long, stick-straight, enhanced with extensions, especially in a different color, such as red, to give your hair a two-toned look. Or—if you're channeling your inner Snooks—gathered at the crown into a pouf.

The eyes. Smoky, dramatic, loads of liner . . . even on the beach. And mile-long lashes, even if you have to glue them on.

Adornments. Tats, piercings—they're the icing on the Guidette cake. Don't go overboard and cover every inch with artwork or holes;

you'll look like a circus freak show. Personally,
I love a belly-button ring and a fire-breathing
dragon tattoo. You can't get hotter than that.

RULE 45: NEVER RUSH PERFECTION

Some women can get ready for a night out in five minutes
flat. Me? I need two and a half hours . . . minimum. And
that is not even as long as some of the ladies in my house
take—Sammi swears she holds the record (three-plus
hours). I know that sounds like a long time to prep and
primp, but it's all part of the Guidette "ritual" of getting
ready. It's unwinding; getting your head in the game. I like
to take a long, hot, sensual shower—literally wash off all
the shit from the day and shed any anxiety or negativity.
I let it all flow down the drain! Then comes choosing the
right outfit and getting your body, your hair, your makeup,
your nails polished to perfection. None of this can be
skipped or skimped on; it takes time to look not just good,
but gorgeous. Do you think Leonardo fucking rushed or
cut corners when he was painting *The Mona Lisa*?

So here's how it goes:

8:30 P.M.

I jump in the shower and make sure I'm fully shaved and
my hair is well washed—if you take your time lathering,
rinsing, lathering up again, you ensure volume. Bigger
the better, I always say, when it comes to men and hair.

9 P.M.

After the shower and before I dry off, I rub on baby oil from the neck down. It's better than lotion for moisturizing; your skin just drinks it in, and it makes your entire body feel (and smell!) like a baby. After I let the oil sit for a few minutes, I towel off.

9:30 P.M.

I rub in leave-in conditioner and a dime-size amount of gloss in my hair, working it through the ends. I take a comb and work out all the tangles so I am starting with a sleek foundation.

9:45 P.M.

Time to blow-dry it straight (see how-tos on page 186).

10:05 P.M.

After my hair is dry, I put it up with a clip so it's out of the way. Then I put bronzer lotion all over to get a deep glow. I let it sit in for at least fifteen minutes before I put my clothes on (or it will smudge all over everything). In the meantime, I put on my makeup and fake eyelashes.

10:25 P.M.

Time to get dressed. I have spent several minutes pre-shower deciding what I want to wear. I recommend doing a try-on. You think something will look good together, then you put it on and it looks like shit. You need to evaluate your options before settling on the perfect look for the night.

10:45 P.M.

I put on deodorant and perfume. I might also take a flat iron to my hair if it's not behaving or it's super hot and sticky out. Humidity will make you poodle up, so it's good to be prepared. Other times, I'll use a curling iron to give it volume. Spritz on hairspray to hold. If you have humidity problems like I did on Season 1, get a Keratin protein treatement on your hair! It works wonders.

10:55 P.M.

I spray a shimmer spray tan instant bronzer on all my exposed skin and finish it off by putting on my jewelry, shoes, and packing a small purse with essentials. Good to go!

RULE 46: IF YOU'RE THE TYPE OF GIRL TO GET IN A BRAWL, KEEP YOUR NAILS SHORT

I had to learn this the hard way—multiple times. I have a knack for getting into fistfights with females (and the occasional guy; right, Mike?), and when a long fake nail snaps off, it's agony. I literally see stars. I'd rather get punched in the face by some chick than have a nail rip off. It takes months to heal, and that process is horrible and painful. If your own nails are stubs and you decide to go with fake ones, it's best to have a pro apply them. It's expensive and there's a lot of upkeep involved as they start to grow out from the cuticle, but it's worth it.

FAKE NAILS 101

....

If you do decide to DIY, my manicurist, Danny, recommends the following:

Step 1: Take off any polish from your real nails and clip/file them short. The surface should be clean and buffed before you apply the fake nails.

Step 2: Get yourself a fake-nail kit that comes with nails in all different sizes. Lay them out and separate them so you know which ones will fit on each finger. You want the fake nail to precisely match the size of your real nail.

Step 3: Apply a small drop of nail glue to your real nail and press the fake nail down on it, holding the nail firm for three to five seconds. Repeat for each nail.

Step 4: Using a nail clipper, cut the size of the nail to the length you want. File it into shape and make sure all the edges are smooth. The longer the nails are, the more likely they are to fall off/tear off—so skip the dragon-lady look if you want them to last.

Step 5: Apply base coat, polish, and topcoat. Your nails should stay for a few days.

RULE 47: HAIR EXTENSIONS ARE A GIRL'S BEST FRIEND

I couldn't live without 'em. My girlfriend Dina Altrui from Maximus applies over 150 strands to my head using a fused keratin process—basically, it hot-glues the hair extensions to your own hair. It's amazing; feels exactly like my hair because it's real human hair, and it lasts for three to six months, so I don't have to worry about it. You can wash it and style it just like your real hair. In my case, I wanted copper highlights, and my own hair is fine and that much color would fry it. So Dina fused in the extensions and made me a freakin' redhead! Love it! And if I want to change my mind and go back to brunette, there's no damage to deal with.

The DIY clip-on hair extensions you find in beauty supply stores are less permanent but equally fun. Regular hair extensions cannot be added and removed when you feel like it because the stylist must glue, braid, sew, or weave them in. Clip-ons have no long-term commitment, which is why the girls at the Shore use them to pump up the volume, add length to hair or contrasting color (like hot pink!) when they're going out partying. In Season 1 I was all about dark hair and platinum extensions (kind of sexy badass skunk?). Here's Dina's tips on how to do it right:

Step 1: Clip-on extensions come in lots of colors and textures, and in different widths. The pieces of hair are called "wefts." You'll need to do this process once or twice to figure out how many wefts you need. Some are made to wrap around the entire head (they have several clips to hold them in place); others are just single strands you clip in for "highlights" at the sides.

Also, buy only real human hair—not synthetic. Real hair can be washed, styled, curled, flat-ironed, etc. If you try to use heat on fake hair, it will melt. The real stuff is more pricey, but worth it.

Step 2: Using a comb, and starting about an inch above the ears, part the hair around the back of the head just below the crown and to the other ear. Clip up the hair above the part so it's out of the way. You're going to be applying the extensions under and into your real hair.

Step 3: Before applying the extension, tease the roots— it will keep the clip from slipping.

Step 4: Open the clips, insert the extension in your own hair just above the roots, then close the clips down to secure. Let down a section of your own hair to cover, then part another section and apply more extensions if you wish, until all the hair is down and blended in.

RULE 48: YOU SHOULD ALWAYS BE "TWO-FACED"— ONE FOR DAY, ONE FOR NIGHT

Never overdo your A.M. face—unless you want someone to mistake you for a ho. I keep it simple: light brown eyeliner, mascara, small amount of bronzer, light pale pink for blush, and a nude lip.

But when it comes to nighttime, I pump up the color and go for drama. The key is to blend, blend, blend. You want to look like a temptress . . . not trailer-park trash. I do the typical Guidette face: lined brows, fake lashes, a smoky eye, darker bronzer that has a little shine to it, dark pink blush, and a pale pink lip. The lighter lip balances out the drama going on up top.

MAKE-OUT-PROOF MAKEUP

I like to leave my mark on a man . . . but I don't think any guy appreciates makeup all over his face, neck, stomach . . . you fill in the blank. Here's how to keep it intact even in the heat of smushing:

LIPSTICK THAT DOESN'T KISS OFF

Reapplying all night long is a pain in the ass. I expect my lipstick to last through drinks, eating dinner, swapping spit with my guy. Many makeup companies have created lipsticks that are specially formulated to stay on for hours—you can't get it off unless you use a sandblaster. The only negative: they tend to make your lips feel dry, so you'll need to apply gloss frequently. You can also get staying power from a traditional lip pencil, lipstick, and gloss. First off, give the lips a little balm for moisture. Blot. Line lips. Blot. Apply lipstick. Blot. Get the picture? The blotting will remove any excess product and leave behind a hint of stain. Finish with a little clear gloss in the center of the bottom lip.

EYES THAT DON'T RUN

I don't know about you, but I don't want any guy mistaking me for a rabid raccoon. Start clean: oil or dirt on your face can lead to a makeup meltdown. You can use a primer in the eye area as a base, or just pat loose powder onto your lids before the shadow. Use a brush or applicator to blend the color around the eye, then follow with a sweep of powder under the lower lashes to set it. You should also make sure that your mascara is waterproof and long-lasting (some can last for eighteen hours) before you pile it on.

FOUNDATION THAT STAYS PUT

I completely understand if you need a little coverage to look flawless—I sure as hell do. Foundation, tinted moisturizer, and concealer are designed to match your skin tone—so they tend to leave a nice orangey-brown stain on everything they touch. Like his pillows . . . or his penis. Look for products with as little oil content as possible. Matte makeup has much more staying power. Dust over your whole face with a sheer powder to set the makeup in place. You can also carry some blotting tissues in your purse for a quick pat-down.

PERMANENT MAKEUP

Permanent makeup let's you feel pretty and confident—no worries that the morning after, your guy will see you all pale and plucked and think, "That's nasty!" I don't care if you're Miss America, no girl is naturally stunning at 6 A.M. I go to Sharon Grasso (www.permanenttouchcosmetics.com) and she does everything from complete eyebrow replacements, permanent eyeliner or lip liner, to scar correction after breast lifts or augmentations. I also love that I can now jump in the pool or the ocean and my makeup isn't running off my face. It's fairly painless (like tattooing makeup on your face) and worth every penny.

RULE 49: NEVER GO TO BED FEELING DIRTY

I don't care how exhausted or hungover you are, when you get home from partying, you need to clean your face. Letting your makeup sit for another several hours is like begging for a breakout. If you're too tired to do a real wash, then at the very least keep some moist towelettes handy in your nightstand and do a quick wipe-down. Then, when you get up the next afternoon, do a thorough cleanse: wash, exfoliate, tone, moisturize. Dr. Stephen T. Greenberg—the plastic surgeon who did my boob job—developed an amazing skin-care line (www.cosmeticsurgeoninajar.com) that keeps my face looking fresh and glowing. He tells me to get enough sleep (at least seven hours a night), protect my face with sunscreen, and drink as much water as possible every day to hydrate. He also recommends laying off the smokes, reducing stress, and working out regularly. I don't think it's too much to ask. I don't want my face looking like a fucking shar-pei when I'm thirty.

RULE 50: YOU CAN NEVER BE TOO RICH OR TOO TAN

Baby, it's all about the bronze. That's why I created JWOWW Black Bronzer Indoor/Outdoor Tanning Lotion! At the *Shore*, you will never, I repeat, NEVER see a pale-faced/white-assed Guido or Guidette. To us, tanning is a religion. The majority of the Guido population lives on the East Coast, and when it's summer, we love to be in the sun. Our days are spent on the beach and at beach parties, pools, barbecues, soaking up the rays. During the fall, winter, and spring months, we go to the tanning salon to keep the color up. Cold weather is no excuse to let your tan fade, especially with all the products on the market to help you go for the glow. I recommend always starting fresh: exfoliate your skin to expose the top layer, and shave before rather than after tanning to remove dead skin. Both will help you tan evenly.

JWOWW'S TANNING TIPS

Never skip the SPF. Even though you are trying to tan, you should still wear sunscreen. Go without, and I promise you, you will burn. You will never see any of us on the *Shore* looking like a lobster. That's because we're smart about it; we lube up before we lay out.

Take your time tanning. If you're white as a ghost, do not spend five hours your first day baking. One hour max. You need to gradually build up to a full day of sunning. And FYI, don't think that burning yourself will give you a good "base" for your tan— all it does is destroy your skin.

Avoid the strongest sun. Lucky for my roommates and me, this is just around the time of day we're waking up! The sun is at its hottest between twelve and three—so you should stay in the shade, or at the very least, cover up.

Water will give you a wicked burn. While you're splashing around, the rays are reflected and magnified onto your body. You're feeling cool in the water, so you probably have no idea that you're burning. Wear sunblock every time you hit the waves—even better if it's water-resistant SPF. Reapply every two to three hours.

Fake a bake. If you don't want to lay out on the beach (or don't have the time), fake tans are just as good. If you can afford it, head to a spa or salon where a pro will give you a flawless application for about a hundred bucks. There are other options as well, like airbrush bronzing (they spray a mist of tanner all over your body) or spray tanning in a booth (i.e., Australian Gold). Though the guys in my house seem to make this a daily ritual, I recommend twice a week—otherwise you are in danger of becoming tanorexic.

You can also pick up a self-tanning lotion or spray-on product and DIY at home. For a temp tan, go with a bronzer. This is more like makeup, and comes in powder or moisturizer. When you're done, you can wash the tan away with soap and water. Since I couldn't get the perfect bronze look I liked, I decided to create my own for Australian Gold: JWOWW's Black Bronzer. Not only is the color great, but it smells yummy.

WHAT TO DO IF YOU FUCK UP YOUR SELF-TAN

....

You wanted to look hot for clubbing this weekend, but instead you're sporting streaks, blotches, or orange palms. Don't freak . . . JWOWW can fix it!

TAN TROUBLE 1: YOU HAVE DARK SPOTS ON THE TOPS OF YOUR HANDS AND FEET

Solution: Rub lemon juice on the blotchy areas to lighten them. Cut a lemon in half and rub right onto your skin; works like magic. In the future, always exfoliate first. The skin on your hands and feet tends to be dry and soaks up the self-tanner more than the rest of your body.

TAN TROUBLE 2: YOU HAVE A BROWN STREAK DOWN THE BACK OF YOUR LEG

Solution: Break out the Windex and scrub with a sponge. The self-tanner will wash away. If you have streaks all over your body, you can soak in a tub of water and baking soda for half an hour; use a body scrub to help slough it off.

TAN TROUBLE 3: YOU HAVE DARK KNUCKLES

Solution: Apply some white toothpaste to them. Let sit for several minutes, then rinse.

TAN TROUBLE 4: YOUR TAN IS UNEVEN

Solution: Use a little concealer everywhere you oopsed—like your face, neck, and chest. If it's really bad, you can pick up a sunless tan remover (they come in little towels) to wipe away the mistakes. Just follow the instructions on the packaging.

TAN TROUBLE 5: YOUR PALMS ARE THE COLOR OF ORANGINA

Solution: Sprinkle some baking soda onto a damp washcloth and rub, rub, rub. If you're not planning on going out in public for a day or two, you're in luck: the outer layer of skin on your hands sheds off quickly—and the color will come off with it. You can prevent this problem down the road by wearing gloves when you apply the self-tanner, or just washing your hands lots of times with hot and soapy water when you're done.

RULE 51: HAIR BELONGS ON YOUR HEAD ... NOWHERE ELSE

There are many ways to defuzz and defur, so there is never a reason you should have stubbly legs, hairy pits, or a girl stache. As for the types who prefer to go natural and let it all hang out . . . good luck getting a guy to go exploring in that jungle!

WAXING

Slightly torturous but highly effective. A pro warms up wax then spreads it over your skin in the direction the hair grows. Once it cools—and those little hairs are stuck in there—she applies a strip and quickly rips it off, yanking the hairs out by the roots. If that sounds like it hurts like hell . . . it does. I have heard grown women scream when getting their bikini area done. But it usually gets easier every time you do it (which is about every three to four weeks; the hair has to grow about a quarter of an inch, and you become desensitized (or just wise up and take a few shots of tequila before the procedure).

TWEEZING

If your brows are looking a little like Oscar the Grouch these days, a tweezer is your best friend. They come in lots of shapes and sizes (round, square, pointed, slanted). In my opinion, the needle-nose ones are best for removing stubborn stubble. Start by brushing the eyebrow hair in the direction of the hair growth. If you're afraid of pain, it helps to take a warm shower first or hold a hot washcloth over your brows before you start; this will open up the pores and make it easier to get the hair out. Make sure you tweeze in the direction of hair growth, and pull each hair one at a time. You can also tweeze stray hairs on your upper lip, chin, and bikini line.

SHAVING

First, find a razor that you like: some come with with lubricated strips, pivoting heads, and multiblades, while others are just pretty colors with fun names like Venus or Daisy. Totally up to you. Never shave your skin dry. You need to first let it soften in a bath or shower from the heat and moisture. And be sure to exfoliate first: dead skin will clog up the blades and you won't get as close a shave. When you're doing your legs, shave up from the ankles since this is the direction the hair grows. When you do your pits, you'll need to shave in every direction and check in a mirror to make sure you got it all.

LASER HAIR REMOVAL

I am all about this technique. It can be pricey, but let me tell you, it is well worth it. You need only four treatments total. One treatment every six weeks and you never have to worry about shaving again. I go back once a year for a treatment, but that's about it. You will notice a huge difference after the first treatment, and by the third, there's barely any new growth.

BLEACHING

An alternative to hair removal, it lasts about two or three weeks. It'll lighten the hair so it's harder to see, but you'll still feel fuzzy.

DEPILATORY CREAMS AND LOTIONS (E.G., NAIR)

These leave skin smooth but they usually stink and can irritate sensitive skin. They also last only a week or two.

ELECTROLYSIS

A professional usually does this permanent hair removal. One hair is zapped out at a time.

EPILATORS

A machine that yanks the hair out, roots and all. It lasts one to six weeks.

RULE 52: EVERY GIRL SHOULD KNOW HOW TO DO A PERFECT BLOW JOB

Get your mind out of the toilet—I am talking about hair. If you become a pro at this, you can do it in under twenty. My *Shore* mates and I would never dream of hitting the clubs without hair that's straight, sleek, shiny, and larger than life.

STEP 1: Wash and condition hair normally. Towel dry; hair should be damp, not wet.

STEP 2: Using a wide-tooth comb, detangle hair; apply leave-in conditioner (to protect hair from heat of dryer) and any other styling products (I like a shine enhancer).

STEP 3: If hair is still dripping wet, use your fingers to remove excess moisture before you start the blow out or let hair air dry for a few minutes.

STEP 4: Divide the hair into three sections, two at the sides and one at the back. Clip the sides up (to get them out of your way). Now take a section of hair at the back, approximately two to three inches wide. Hold the dryer in one hand and the brush in the other. A large round brush is best for getting hair super-smooth.

STEP 5: Beginning at the roots, use the brush to pull the section of hair taut; otherwise moisture stays in the hair shaft and hair will frizz up. Start by drying the underside of the section, gently pulling the brush through to the ends, and lifting out and away from the head.

STEP 6: Once the underside is dry, point the nozzle of the dryer down onto the top side of the hair, at about a forty-five-degree angle. This will smooth and create shine. Again, use the brush to pull the section away from the head, stretching and straightening as you work from roots to ends.

STEP 7: Take your time. Make sure each section is dry and straight before moving onto the next. Once you have finished the bottom, unclip the sides and work on them.

STEP 8: Finish with a light mist of hair spray or shine-spray.

Dear JWOWW:

I partied too hard last night and now I look like crap. How can I hide my hangover with makeup?

The morning after sucks—thank God for makeup! First, you need to get rid of the big, black bags under your eyes. Use ice, cucumber slices, tea bags, a cold spoon, whatever. Next, apply a depuffing eye cream (if you're going to make a habit of getting wasted, you might want to invest in a good one!) under your eyes and on your lids. If you're a lovely shade of green from hurling, put on a tinted moisturizer to even out your skin tone and dab a little blush on the apples of your cheeks. Go easy on the eyes—you don't want to call attention to the fact that they're bloodshot. Stick to a clear mascara and some neutral shadow, just so you look awake.

CHAPTER 9

SMUSHING

RULE 53: NEVER JUDGE A BOOK BY ITS COVER OR
A RELATIONSHIP BY THE FIRST SMUSH

You found a great guy and you're ready to seal the deal. Good for you; have fun getting down to Business. Just be sensible about where you set the bar. If you go in expecting the earth to move the first time you have sex, you'll probably be disappointed. Why? Because it's a rare couple that scores a nine on the Richter scale right out of the gate. I'm not saying it can't happen. I'm just saying that most men, no matter how much shit they talk about being fucking amazing in bed, could use a road map.

To be fair, there's a hell of a lot of pressure to perform well. You both want the first time to be perfect—or at the least, the stuff that porno flicks are made of. But you've probably been drinking, not to mention building this moment up in your heads. It can be awkward, uncomfortable, and a huge downer (especially if he can't get it up!). So your "perfect" night turns to perfect shit, and you're left wondering if this relationship stands a chance.

I set reasonable sexpectations for the first time. I like to think of it as getting-to-know-you sex. You're learning what each partner likes/doesn't like and what buttons to push. There's trial and error involved. I also think there's a hell of a lot of emotion tied to the first smush. Having sex changes everything and brings up a lot of questions. What does this mean? Where will it lead? Will he still want you once he nails you? With all of this crap rolling around in your brain, it's pretty hard to focus on quality smushing. How the hell are you supposed to enjoy yourself when you're wondering if he'll ever call you after tonight? I guarantee that once you both calm down, it will get easier and better. If it doesn't, see below.

WHAT TO DO IF THE SEX SUCKS

It happens—hopefully not more than once.
But if you two fail to create fireworks in bed,
you have a few options:

SHOW AND TELL

If he has the basic moves down, maybe he just needs a
little guidance to take it to the next level. Tell him what
you like; show him what (and where!) feels good. Don't
bark orders ("Not there! Over here!"), instead purr like
a kitten when he's in the right area and guide his hand
to your hot spots. Different people like different things.
Who knows? Maybe the last chick he was with had an
erogenous zone up her ass? The guy's not psychic: you
have to communicate what turns you on.

DON'T DO IT . . . FOR A WHILE

Ain't nothing like no sex to make you want it and
appreciate it more. If it sucked the first few times, give
it a rest. Then when you can't stand another minute
of teasing and dry-humping, give it another try.
Abstinence can make the heart grow fonder—and his
dick grow harder.

MAKE A MIND–BODY CONNECTION

Sex isn't just about the physical. Sometimes, you need
to feel turned on mentally as well. A lot of times
couples jump into bed with no emotional foreplay.
You don't talk; you don't share your feelings. How the
fuck are you supposed to share an intimate act without
any intimacy? If your sex was off, it might mean you
need to connect in ways not involving being on top of
each other. This is an easy one; just insist on spending
a few hours getting to know each other. Just having

something in common (You both like the Giants! You both watch *Jersey Shore*!) can take your smushing to a whole new level.

WORK OUT

I am not shitting you: experts say exercise can make sex mind-blowing. It stimulates not only the body but also your nerves and brain. Plus it gets blood pumping to all the right places—so you're more excited and receptive (translation: THE BIG O!). I also think it reduces stress and boosts self-esteem. Suggest to your man that you both hit the gym a few hours before you hit the sack and see how things go.

USE YOUR MOUTH

Sometimes smushing can feel like a wrestling match—all arms and hands pawing, clawing, and grabbing. Instead, use your lips, teeth, and tongue to lick, suck, nibble, and kiss. Instant turn-on for both teams!

RUB HIM THE RIGHT WAY

A massage can work miracles for so-so smushing. It loosens up the muscles and makes every inch of him electrified. You do him, then he does you. You can even add self-heating massage oil to start a fire down below.

RULE 54: MEN LOVE A LADY WHO HAS SKILLS

Let's be honest: guys may say they're looking for someone pure and respectable to bring home to Mama, but
they're secretly praying she's a fucking nympho with
a bachelor's degree in banging. A lot of women would
read this as "I have to whore it up for a guy to like me."
Not by a long shot. I am all for practice makes perfect,
but that's with the guy you're seeing—not the entire
college football team. I do not believe in prostituting
myself. I don't sleep around, and I don't have sex before
I am 100 percent ready. I am not—as Snooks would
say—"a loosey goosey." But that doesn't mean I am not
skilled in the art of seduction. Baby, there ain't no better
than JWOWW! And I believe that every woman should
master these six tricks to drive a man wild. There's no
smushing involved (unless he begs, of course . . .).

TEASE HIM

Run your fingers—or your lips—over his entire body,
exploring every inch. You can also blow him. No, not
that type of blow (although that would work, too!); I
mean blow air on his skin in a seductive way. Kind of
like a soft, sexy whistle on his neck, his chest, his stomach, wherever . . .

TALK DIRTY

I'm always down for this one; I think it's incredibly seductive to tell a guy what you're fantasizing he'll do to you, or better yet, what you're going to do to him when you get the chance. Don't say stuff that makes you feel uncomfortable, and keep in mind where you choose to make your dirty declarations. You don't want to embarrass him in front of his family or friends (although in my *Shore* house, they found it pretty damn entertaining). I recommend starting off slow—nothing too hardcore raunchy—and see how he reacts. You don't want to creep him out by going overboard. You want him to think you're sexy . . . not a freak with a fetish!

DRESS UP

Just like you did when you were a kid—only now you're playing stripper, not Snow White! Keep it fresh and fun: surprise him by showing up one night as a naughty schoolgirl; the next as a cop. Ask him what he'd like to see you dressed as, then fulfill his fantasy. But the costume is only half of the equation: you also have to get into the part. If you're playing policeman, "bust him" for being a bad boy: hands behind his head, full pat-down, lock him up in cuffs, and throw away the key while you have your way with him.

PULL OUT THE PROPS

Guys go nuts if they see a girl pleasuring herself with a toy. It makes them think they've got a porno star right in their own bedroom—and they're hypnotized watching you in action. The way I look at it, it's a win-win situation: you get off, and he gets to watch! Come on, ladies, it's the twenty-first century, and being shy is no longer allowed!

MAKE SOME NOISE

Give him positive feedback when you're fooling around. Pant, moan, groan, howl like a fucking dog in heat—show him he's hitting all the right notes. He'll be incredibly turned on by his ability to bring ecstasy to the opposite sex (aren't they all?). It's like giving him a fucking standing ovation! Personally, I say the louder the better—it's always a good way to piss off the neighbors, too.

TAKE CONTROL

A man—especially one who thinks he's tough—loves it when a girl surprises him and takes the reins. Hold him down by the wrists, back him into a corner, blindfold him, or get on top. Show him who's boss . . . in a sexy, seductive way.

RULE 55: UNLEASH YOUR INNER PORN STAR

The key to a supercharged sex life isn't how much sex you have—it's how much you enjoy it. And that means letting go—unleashing your wild side and getting down with your bad-girl self. A guy will tell you that any girl who is self-confident is also a great lay. I get that some women are shy—if you recall, I wasn't always such a hard-ass, especially not when I was in my early twenties.

Maybe you were brought up to be a "good girl." There is nothing wrong with that—but you also have permission to be a hot woman. The trick is to stop holding yourself back.

DON'T FOCUS ON FLAWS

So what if your thighs jiggle or your ass is fat? Obsessing over it won't make it go away (a personal trainer or lipo might). If you're self-conscious about getting naked, then listen up: no guy is going to get into bed with a magnifying glass. You're the one who's distracted by these small imperfections, not him. He's only interested in getting it in—not getting a close look at your cellulite. Forget about it. And if you can't, then dim the lights or fucking blindfold him! He'll think it's kinky.

WALK AROUND BARE-ASS NAKED

There's nothing like strutting around in the buff to boost your body confidence. I don't recommend this, however, if you have roommates or no shades on your windows (and curious neighbors). At the very least, go to bed naked and get used to how it feels. The more comfortable you are in your own skin, the more relaxed you'll be when you smush.

GET IN THE MOOD

Read a raunchy romance novel, watch a steamy porno flick, take a warm bubble bath, and let your anxiety melt away. Basically, you need to get out of your head and into "the zone." Light candles, crank up some sexy tunes.

PICTURE YOURSELF AS SOMEONE ELSE

How would a badass movie star like Angelina Jolie or Megan Fox act in bed? How would she think, act, speak, and react? Practice channeling this "character" as though you were acting out a part in a play. You won't feel as self-conscious because you won't be you . . . technically.

FRESHEN UP

You'll feel sexier if your skin is soft, dewy, and smells delicious. Shave your arms, pits, and even down there so it feels smooth as a baby's ass. I like to take a long hot shower and lube myself up with baby oil. There's something very sensual about running your hands all over your body . . . makes you feel nasty before he even walks in the door.

RULE 56: IT DOESN'T TAKE MUCH TO GROSS A GUY OUT

Most of them turn into squeamish little girls at the mere mention of your time of the month, B.O., or body zits. They want to think of you as perfection on a pedestal—so why shatter that image? Do everything you can to keep the goddess rep going—and just beware of the little things that might freak them out. Sometimes they're easy to see and fix (like get a wax, will you?). Other times, they're more about your attitude (you constantly nag, bring up your ex, act like you're too good for him).

TEN PHYSICAL THINGS THAT TURN A GUY OFF

These are easy to remedy and prevent with a little attention to detail.

1. **Hairy legs, arms, pits, a jungle growing down there**. Shave it, wax it, mow it. Whatever you have to do to de-fur, do it! You don't want to remind him of a werewolf or worse, his uncle Mauro.

2. **Dirty, greasy hair**. He doesn't want you oiling up his pillows.

3. **Skank**. B.O. is simply not acceptable.

4. **Unattractive underwear**. As previously discussed—he'll feel like he's fondling his nonna. If you want a man in your pants, then you have to up your game when it comes to panties.

5. **Bad breath**. Pop a mint, brush your teeth, floss! No guy wants to kiss you and taste the garlic bread you had at dinner.

6. **Bad skin/body acne**. I know some girls have a problem. But a facialist or a derm doc can help you get zits under control before your pimples send him packing.

7. **Cold sore**. Ain't nothing like a herpes to make a guy run for the hills! Remember Pauly meeting a girl on the beach then backing away when he saw a sore?

8. **Your period**. Guys just can't deal with the mess—even if they say they're cool with it (and wanna have sex), they're freaked out. I recommend going into seclusion till you're off the rag. It's only a few days . . . deal.

9. **Earwax**. Do you not own a Q-tip? No man wants to put his tongue in and taste candle.

10. **Nose hairs/unibrow**. You think a guy doesn't notice stray hairs springing up where they shouldn't be? Tweeze before you go out with him.

TEN NONPHYSICAL THINGS THAT
TURN A GUY OFF

These are more complicated because they involve fixing how your brain is wired. You need to recognize these in yourself and admit you do them so you can get control.

1. **You make weird noises during sex**. And not good ones: I'm talking whistling, honking, clucking, hissing. He wants to be banging a wild animal—not a barnyard beast. Hit the mute button, will ya?

2. **You're obsessed with your ex**. No guy wants to be constantly compared to someone you used to smush. Make it a rule to NEVER mention his name when you're getting down to Business. It's like using a fire extinguisher on his dick.

3. **You behave like a conceited bitch**. Yes, Guidos like to brag—but they don't want their women to be strutting around thinking their shit don't stink. I am all for projecting confidence, but if you're constantly announcing how hot you are—and how no one can measure up to you—a guy is gonna do his very best to prove you wrong.

4. **You're a constant complainer**. The pasta he made you is too al dente; the roses he bought you are the

wrong color; you hate his hair, his roommates, his car. You bitch and criticize—and you wonder why he's sticking his dick in some other chick.

5. **You're a Debbie Downer**. What fun is it to be with a woman who is constantly moping, sulking, crying her eyes out? I know circumstances sometimes put you in a blue mood you can't shake—your pet hamster died or your boss skipped over you for promotion. That's understandable. But if you're always seeing the glass as half empty and dragging your ass around in self-imposed misery, your man is gonna take cover from the dark clouds. He doesn't want to be your therapist . . . he wants to bang you. 'Nuf said.

6. **You talk too much**. Seriously: you never shut up. Your mouth is always running a hundred miles a minute, and with that constant commentary, he can't get a word in (or even hear himself think). What can you do about it? Either take a vow of silence or, at the very least, practice your listening skills. An occasional "So what's your opinon?" will do wonders for your relationship.

7. **You're a nervous wreck**. I understand having a few phobias—personally, I freak at the sight of frogs, mice, bugs in general—but if you're afraid of your own shadow, a guy's gonna get scared off. What are you worried about? Is your concern coming from insecurity?

Work on building your strength and confidence and projecting positive thoughts. Fear will turn your life to shit—and of that, I would be very, very afraid.

8. **You're too serious, too fast**. You've been dating only a week, and you've already bought matching Mr. and Mrs. T-shirts. Big no-no. Even if things are going well, don't assume anything about your future until there is a ring on your finger. Guys hate to be rushed into a relationship. Go slow; keep it cool and casual. Don't turn the screws. If he smells commitment before he's ready, he'll be gone faster than you can say, "I do."

9. **You spend every cent you have**. A girl who is constantly broke and can't curb her spending habits is a major turnoff. An occasional shopping spree with your girlfriends is fine; $50K in maxed-out credit cards isn't. It shows a lack of control and responsibility, and he's gonna get sick of paying your tab. Of course, if you want to shower him with gifts, your guy won't protest too much. But he will freak if your landlord tosses your ass out on the street and you ask to move in. Grow up and save up.

10. **You act immature**. You can't go to sleep without the lights on, you have a collection of stuffed animals, and your idea of phone sex is babbling baby talk. Some guys might find this cute; most will want to hurl. There's nothing adorable about a woman who acts

like a toddler (including the temper tantrums). It's fine to play games or watch the occasional Scooby-Doo cartoon together, but if all you do is crawl into his lap with your teddy bear, he's gonna start to feel like your daddy, not your boyfriend. Men want a mature woman in the bedroom—not jailbait.

RULE 57: THINK OUTSIDE THE BOX IN THE BEDROOM

As I've said before, creativity and "mixing it up" are the key to a happy long-term relationship. Employ costumes, props, switch up the scenery—anything you can think of to get his heart racing. There is no excuse for a boring, lackluster sex life. Need inspiration? Why not . . .

- Dress up like a nurse and give him a sponge bath.
- Suggest a game of strip poker—winner gets all the foreplay!
- Tie him up. Or break out the whip. "Have you been a bad boy lately?"
- Serve yourself up for dessert. Whipped cream, chocolate sauce, edible undies . . .
- Take pictures or make a video—just make sure it's for your eyes only.
- Use heated and flavored massage oils—in every nook and cranny.
- Go shopping at an adults-only toy store together.
- Do a sexy striptease.
- Have sex somewhere unexpected: the kitchen

table, the hot tub, the shower, the dressing room at Macy's (hee hee!).

- Watch an erotic movie: *Basic Instinct, Wild Orchid, 9 1/2 Weeks, Debbie Does Dallas* . . .
- Type a turn-on: send a raunchy e-mail or text (just make sure he won't get in trouble at work!).
- Buy a book about sexual positions . . . and work your way through all of them.
- Have sex at a different time of day: the middle of the night, early in the A.M., on your lunch hour.
- Feed him aphrodisiacs: oysters, chocolate, champagne, Viagra . . .
- Seduce him with scent: fragrant candles or flowers around the house, perfume behind your ears, a lasagna in the oven.

DEAR JWOWW:

My guy wants a threesome as a present for his twenty-fifth. What should I do?

Personally, I would never do it. You will never catch my ass sharing my man, no fucking way. But if it doesn't bother you—or if it turns you on—then I say go for it. You only live once. Just make sure you're not being bullied into it. Are you sure you're cool with the idea of your man getting it on with another woman—while

> you watch or participate? I would set some
> serious ground rules, as in "You can touch,
> fondle, and kiss the bitch—but you cannot fuck
> her!" I'd also make sure condoms are used and
> that your guy isn't secretly hot for the third
> wheel. You want this to be a one-night-only
> event—not an invitation for him to cheat on
> you whenever he fucking feels like it.

RULE 58: HONESTY IS THE BEST POLICY . . . EVEN IF IT'S SOMETHING YOU'RE NOT PROUD OF

No one is a saint (myself included) and you're bound to have skeletons in your closet you'd rather not reveal. But certain issues merit full disclosure—especially if you're about to smush. I feel like I'd wanna know these things, so I owe it to a guy to show him the same respect.

STDS

I would flip script if someone I was seeing had something and didn't tell me. Man up and give it to me straight: I'll be more pissed off if I wind up catching something that could have been avoided. If you have an STD—or had one in the recent past—I think it's always best to bring it up before you get too sexual with a guy. Basically, if you're thinking about doing the deed—and there are naked body parts already involved—you should have the talk. I know it's not an easy discussion—about as pleasant as a root canal—but it's the right thing to do if you respect him. You could start by saying, "Before we smush, I want us to talk about protection because I have an STD." If he doesn't know much about what you have/had, then fill him in on how it's transmitted and how to avoid catching it. If you're on medication or were treated in the past, then say so. You don't have to share every nasty detail of how you caught it ("I slept with about twenty different guys in college—could have been any of them . . .). Just say you wanted to be honest and make him comfortable with the situation. If he isn't a total douchebag, he'll appreciate you coming clean and caring enough to protect him. If you've already had sex—and are feeling like a total bitch for not being up front—then no time like the present to set the record straight. Encourage him to talk to a doctor and get tested so you can get back to Business without any hesitation.

YOU'VE NEVER DONE "IT" BEFORE

Being a virgin is not something to be ashamed of. It shows you take smushing very seriously—and you don't just give it up for any loser. Most guys will be totally turned on by the fact that they get to "deflower" you—it's a huge honor, believe me. They'll be bragging about it for weeks. But there also may be a few who freak out at the huge responsibility of being "your first." The fact that you've waited this long leads a guy to assume you're holding out for someone special, maybe even "The One," which could scare the crap out of them. That's major pressure.

Being a virgin is not something I would casually mention over linguini and clam sauce, but if he asks how many men you've been with, you have an opening. You could simply say, "I'm very choosy." The less said, the better. And don't get into your reasons; e.g., you were painfully shy in high school or once weighed 250-plus pounds and didn't have many offers. Your reasons are your reasons. But I would also advise you not to let him pressure you. Don't give it up until you're 100 percent sure you're ready. It's not something you can ever get back. You have no idea how many women wish they could!

PROTECTION

If you're old enough to have sex, you're old enough to talk about it. I believe you need to get this topic out in the open ASAP. Buddy, if you're going to be smushing me on a regular basis, you better have a game plan of protection. If it's a one-nighter or something I know will not amount to long term, then I do not negotiate: no glove, no love. But when we're serious and exclusive, then we need to talk about getting tested, birth control, and what it means to be fucking me (i.e., your dick is off-limits to any other women). If I'm going unprotected, then I want a guarantee (in writing if necessary) that you are (a) clean and (b) intend on staying that way. Is it really so much to ask? If a guy can't commit to one partner, then don't be an idiot: keep condoms in your nightstand. If he doesn't like it, tough shit. You have no idea what skank he's hooking up with when you're not around, and you can't take chances.

YOU'VE HAD SEX WITH THE SAME SEX

A girl that likes both the hole *and* the pole? Most guys will think they hit the jackpot. Do not stress about sharing this info: he'll probably chalk it up to a wild, drunken adventure and secretly hope it's an invitation for a threesome (NOT!). If it wasn't a big deal, then don't make it into one. But if you're bi, a guy might worry he's not going to be enough for you. Be honest about your sexuality so he knows what he's down for. He might be more open-minded than you think. But if you don't tell him—and he hears it from some whore you once made out with in a club—it's not gonna be pretty.

RULE 59: DON'T SMUSH AND TELL

In my *Shore* house, it's hard to keep secrets—especially when the cameras are rolling 24/7. Everybody knows everybody's business, like it or not. The minute Vinny pounded Snooki, we all heard about it. But in general, I don't believe it's a good thing to dish the deets about your sex life. Even if you trust the person you're telling (i.e., your BFF), it could get back to your partner—and you don't know how it will make him or her feel. The guys at the *Shore* are much worse than the girls when it comes to gossip; they sit around like the chicks on *Sex and the City* comparing fucking notes over breakfast. I'm sorry: TMI. I do not need to know what acrobatic acts that bitch did to you in bed. And if I were her, I'd be pretty pissed off that you're broadcasting it. In my opinion, sex is an intimate act between two people and it should remain that way. If you spill, you're compromising the trust. Occasionally, you might need your friend or sister's advice, and that's okay. But if you're telling to brag, shock, or make someone else feel like shit . . . keep it to yourself. It certainly didn't help John Mayer's love life and it sure as hell won't help yours.

Dear JWOWW:

My boyfriend's mother walked in on us having wild sex. Should I say something to her?

You're lucky it wasn't *your* mother who walked in—that would be a whole other pile of shit to deal with! I say his mom, his problem. If he's a big boy, then she probably assumes he's doing the nasty with girls. You just got caught in the act, which is embarrassing, yes, but not the end of the world. You're talking to a woman who dated a guy who was living in his mother's basement. You don't think she heard some crazy noises coming from downstairs? I would forget it ever happened. Don't bring it up if you go to dinner, and certainly don't make it a point to apologize. Chances are she's even more embarrassed than you are and would like to erase the image of you banging her baby boy from her mind entirely.

RULE 60: THE MOST IMPORTANT ONE OF ALL: EVERY WOMAN HAS IT IN HER TO "WOWW"

I wasn't always JWOWW; for most of my life I was simply Jenni. I made a conscious decision to rethink and repackage who I was and to level the playing field. It's what landed me at the Shore and made me the kick-ass bitch I am today—in a good way. No matter what crazy shit goes down in our house or on the scene (and at times it's pretty fucking insane), I'm okay. Why? Because I respect myself and my choices, and I live by my own rules, no one else's.

Recently I had a minor bump in the road with Perfection and I decided to leave him. I wasn't thinking logically . . . just being my hot headed self. I threw out all my rules and got angry at him one day for no reason and I crossed the line. Even though I call him Perfection, some things about him are flawed. There is a certain situation I don't like in his life, and on some days I can't deal with it. When we first got together I didn't mind because I wasn't in love with him. But as time goes on, some things are harder to accept as feelings are involved. I can't help it; I'm only human.

After I walked out, he called me and said he was sorry. I accepted, but then we fought all over again. We both did each other wrong and needed to get over some things. I'm still not 100 percent with him, and I don't know if I ever will be. Bridges were burned, things were said, lies were told, and tears were shed. There's tension at this moment. But love, compassion, and most important, communication, can save us.

So, I will have to let time heal all and see if we can repair our relationship or just accept we cannot and move on. I'm actually proud of myself for standing my ground on this and being strong. I am not just telling you to live by my rules . . . I am living by them, too.

Now I'm asking you to do the same. You know what the basic rules are; it's time to have the balls to put them to work for you. All talk and no action won't change your life, help you forget your ex, or land the Guido of your dreams. You have to wake up one morning and decide this is what you want—and this is how you're going to make it happen.

Take what you've learned in this book and apply it to your life. You don't have to do it all at once. Just get the cleavage and the confidence down and the rest will follow.

They'll never know what hit 'em . . .

ACKNOWLEDGMENTS

Many thanks to . . .

My family and friends: Mom, Joey (my sidekick), Kate (always there for me), "Perfection" (who loves me for me), Nicole (my Boo Boo), Yanice, Jacqui Rose.

My amazing managers, Paul and Abbey; my *Jersey Shore* family; MTV; and 495 Productions.

To all the old boyfriends who gave me the ammo to write this and the experiences to make me a woman.

Thank you to the publishing team that helped create this book: Sheryl Berk, my cowriter, for capturing my voice in print—thank you; Amy Bendell, my editor at HarperCollins, Lisa Sharkey, and the incredible folks at HarperCollins, including Liate Stehlik, Lynn Grady, Jean Marie Kelly, Shawn Nicholls, Seale Ballenger, Shelby Meizlik, James Iacobelli, and Richard Aquan for giving me this opportunity; my lit agent extraordinaire, Frank Weimann.

Thank you to my team of experts for setting me off in the right direction: At Maximus Salon: Dina Altrui, my hair stylist; Christine Kinney, my stylist; Raquel, my makeup artist; and Richard Calcasola, the owner of the salon. Jeni Luciani, my wardrobe stylist. Dr. Stephen Greenberg, my plastic surgeon.